# Yes, Lord!

## Harald Bredesen
## With Pak King

16pt

# Copyright Page from the Original Book

Published by Regal
From Gospel Light
Ventura, California, U.S.A.
*www.regalbooks.com*
Printed in the U.S.A.

Library of Congress Cataloging-in-Publication Data
Bredesen, Harald
Yes, Lord, by Harald Bredesen, with Pat King.
p. illus. cm.
ISBN 978-08307-4535-7 (hard cover)
BR1725.B683 A3
266'0092'4 B
72091776

1 2 3 4 5 6 7 8 9 10 / 10 0 9 08 07

Rights for publishing this book outside the U.S.A. or in non-English languages are administered by Gospel Light Worldwide, an international not-for-profit ministry. For additional information, please visit www.glww.org, email info@glww.org, or write to Gospel Light Worldwide, 1957 Eastman Avenue, Ventura, CA 93003, U.S.A.

# TABLE OF CONTENTS

*To my wife—the other half of my soul.*

# PREFACE

Harald Bredesen died on December 29, 2006, at the age of 88. Three days before, Bredesen suffered a head injury after falling at his home in Escondido, California. He was hospitalized but never regained consciousness. *Yes, Lord!* tells the story of this unassuming, faithful follower of Christ who fought against following in his preacher father's footsteps and ended up influencing televangelists, Hollywood actors, world leaders and others.

Born in North Dakota in 1918 and raised in Iowa, Bredesen moved to New York City in 1944. There he launched an unconventional and far-reaching ministry, eventually becoming known as the father of the charismatic renewal. Early on, a persistent Bredesen persuaded President Harry S Truman to sponsor a Sunday School campaign, helped launch a New Testament-style church that emphasized prophetic revelations, and led M.G. "Pat" Robertson into the baptism of the Holy Spirit. "Harald was always ready to say yes to God," Robertson said. "He spent literally hours crying out for more of the Holy Spirit."

Having met Bredesen in New York, Robertson accompanied him to a dinner meeting with Ruth Stafford Peale, wife of *Guideposts* magazine founder Norman Vincent Peale. That dinner meeting led to *Guideposts* editor John L. Sherrill writing *They Speak with OtherTongues,* one of the most influential books in the early days of the charismatic renewal. The title is a phrase that Bredesen coined.

Bredesen worked with Robertson to found the Christian Broadcasting Network, served on its board of directors, and for a time hosted his own television show, *Charisma.* He eventually came to be called "Mr. Charisma."

"Harald Bredesen was the original charismatic, the earliest post-World War II neo-Pentecostal from a mainline denomination to receive the Pentecostal experience and remain in his church," said historian Vinson Synan. "His influence on Pat Robertson and others was epochal. When he prayed in tongues, it was with power and authority."

Pat Boone was also influenced by Bredesen. At a pivotal moment in Boone's career, Bredesen and Boone prayed together during a now-legendary walk on Mulholland Drive in Los Angeles. Days later, Bredesen warned Boone not to become "unequally yoked," but he had no clue that Boone was about to sign a recording contract with unbelievers.

Whether it was standing face to face with a superstar singer or praying in tongues aloud on a Brooklyn bus, Bredesen never dodged acting on what he believed God asked of him. An appointment with a world leader didn't dissuade him either. Janet St. Pierre, at one time Bredesen's secretary and later an assistant to Boone, recalled that Bredesen once asked Boone to immediately write a letter of introduction for him. Bredesen was in Egypt and believed God wanted him to meet with President Anwar Sadat. He thought the Egyptian leader would respond to Boone. It worked. Bredesen spent several hours with Sadat, praying with him and conducting a television interview.

Bredesen gained audiences with other world leaders, including President Ronald Reagan and Canadian Prime Minister Pierre Trudeau. One time, Bredesen, Boone and evangelist George Otis, Sr. met with then-California Governor Ronald Reagan. Otis told Reagan that if he remained faithful, he would someday occupy 1600 Pennsylvania Avenue. With Otis on one side of Reagan and Bredesen on the other, the group joined hands and prayed.

Bredesen is credited with prompting the call for prayer that Jimmy Carter, Anwar Sadat and Menachem Begin sent out at the beginning of their historic Camp David meetings. He later founded the Prince of Peace Foundation, which honors international peacemakers with a Christian counterpart of the Nobel Peace Prize. Sadat, Mother Teresa and Jordan's King Hussein have been the recipients.

Until his last year, Bredesen never slowed his pace. "Harald Bredesen reflected the father heart of God with rare excellence," evangelist Ed Silvoso said. "He took time to speak into my life and pray for me. I was blessed beyond measure to be affirmed and encouraged by this giant."

Jack Hayford, president of the Los Angeles-based International Church of the Foursquare Gospel and pastor of The Church On The Way in Van Nuys, California, said that his friend Bredesen "was among the four or five most pivotal human instruments under God's grace whom He used to influence leaders and impact nations during the mid-1960s to mid-1980s' charismatic renewal."

"Harald Bredesen had an anointing to touch key leaders of the world," recalled Bill Hamon, who co-authored *The Eternal Church* with Bredesen. "He was a real prophet of God."

Reprinted from *Charisma* magazine, March 2007

Used by permission

# INTRODUCTION

Ever wonder what kind of a guy Abraham was?

I mean, can you imagine a character just pulling up stakes in his home town, packing up his dad, his wife, his close relatives, and all his considerable earthly possessions in a big unwieldy caravan, and wandering from country to country—without even knowing where he was going?

Can you imagine this same legendary figure, now an old man, taking his grown son up on a mountain and actually raising a knife to kill him, believing that God had commanded such a terrible thing?

"Yes, Lord."

Have you ever, in your imagination, tried to savor the personality of a man like Moses who obeyed a "voice" coming to him out of a burning bush? A meek man like Moses who would leave his sheep after 40 years of hermit-like existence and dare to approach a powerful world monarch and command him to release Egypt's whole slave population? And then present himself as their "wagonmaster"—to lead more than 2 million people to a country none of them, including Moses, had ever seen?

"Yes, Lord."

Have you ever wondered how Gideon felt when he stood shivering in the night air, looking down at the massive Midianite camp, about to give the order to his "troops"? An order to 300 mystified men to break the earthen pitchers in their hands, exposing 300 ridiculous torches, and to blow on their trumpets with all their might—deliberately waking up the thousands of sleeping enemies below?

"Yes, Lord."

Would you like to sit down with incredible old Elijah and ask him if he didn't feel just a little bit foolish (and a whole lot scared) when he challenged the 450 prophets of the heathen god Baal? I mean, can you picture yourself, with thousands of people watching, standing before an altar with a dead ox on it, ordering young men to douse and soak the whole business with water three times—and then shouting into the skies for God to suddenly burn the altar down, without even a match? Mightn't you have felt foolish and scared?

"Yes, Lord."

Well, I think I've known such a man as these.

His name was Harald Bredesen.

Oh, Harald would have cringed at the comparison with these mighty spiritual giants. He was painfully aware of his shortcomings and his many flops, as you're about to read for yourself.

But so was Moses. Remember, he tried his best to get out of going down into Egypt, listing all his obvious drawbacks to God. But when Moses finally got around to saying "Yes, Lord," God did amazing things with him!

Harald is about to tell you how long—how painfully long—it took him to quit trying to work out God's promises with his own schemes and to experience the heady thrill of the yielded Faith Walk.

Sort of reminds me of Abraham. It took him a while, too.

But each time Abraham said "Yes, Lord," God led him into a new miracle—and the Lord *seems* to like Abraham's kind of faith, doesn't He?

I really think that knowing Harald Bredesen was a little like knowing Elijah, too.

Because even after God answered that dramatic and seemingly foolhardy call for fire, consuming the ox, altar and the 450 prophets of Baal—Elijah soon experienced doubt, fear and depression. He ran off into a mountain cave and hid, even asking God to take his life!

It makes me think of the time Harald ... but you'll soon be reading that for yourself.

My point is not that Harald Bredesen was just by nature a spiritual giant. Far from it. He was flesh and blood, strength and weakness, fear and faith—just like me.

The thing that thrilled me about Harald in the several years I knew him was that he was so willing to say "Yes, Lord"—and because of that he lived the wonderful adventure that you're about to share.

He and his remarkable Gen followed in some of the footsteps of Abraham and Sarah—miracles trailed them wherever they went. They *knew* this Jesus whom they spoke about—intimately—and He "worked with them, confirming His word" as they acted upon it.

Best of all, they gave me and thousands of others the realization that there is the potential of Moses, Elijah, Gideon and Jesus in each of us—as we learn, like them, to say "Yes, Lord."

Pat Boone

Jesus whom they spoke

acted upon it.

# 1

Two A.M. I was tired that spring night in 1946, so tired that I sat down on the curb alongside the Empire State Building as I waited for the bus. When it finally pulled up, I took the side seat by the door, leaned back against the window, and closed my eyes. Then it came, a voice low but insistent and frightening. It hadn't come from anyone on the bus but from somewhere inside of me.

I knew it was the Lord, and my stomach turned to jelly at His words. *Preach to the people on this bus.*

"But, Lord, I can't. I'm a Lutheran minister and Lutheran ministers don't preach on buses. It's unheard of. What would Dad think, if he knew? What would my seminary classmates say?"

I could hear the throaty roar of the exhaust as the bus turned onto Lexington Avenue. I could feel the cold metal of the seat frame as I braced my hand against it. But my mind was reflecting on something that had happened 3,500 years ago, when Moses stood on Mount Pisgah. From it he could see a land flowing with milk and honey. He could see it, but he could not enter it. At one crucial point he had failed God.

Earlier this very night, through one of His servants, God had given me a glimpse of the glorious new life He had in store for me. But now it was as if He was saying, "You'll never be able to enter in if you deny Me this one act of obedience."

I thought, "But if I preach, everyone on the bus will think I'm a crazy fanatic." I wondered if an entire future really could hinge on just one act of obedience. "If I do obey, the worst they can do is kill me." The thought offered little comfort.

Shaking with fear and with no idea what I would say, I stood up and grabbed the steel post behind me. There were only eight people on the bus, but it seemed like a thousand. All of them were staring at me. "Lord, please don't ask this of me."

The Lord didn't answer. It was as if He was beside me, awaiting my decision. Finally I took my unwilling soul by the scruff of the neck and said, "Yes, Lord."

I hung onto the steel post for dear life and opened my mouth. He filled it. I found myself speaking with a power I had never known before. Every word was weighted like a pile driver. No one acted as if he might commit mayhem. In fact, everyone sat up and listened. A teenage girl leaned forward, hanging on every word. An old man halfway back began to weep. On my right a large woman was staring at me open-mouthed. I went over to her and asked, "Madam, do you know what I'm talking about?"

"Sure I do. You're saying we got to be born again." Her eyes became like two pieces of glass. Two other eyes, wild, cunning and jackal-like, leered out at me. Suddenly I heard myself saying, "You knew what those words meant once. You were a Christian. But then you had to choose between something you wanted and Christ. Now Satan has you bound hand and foot, and you're demon possessed."

"What if I am? You get away from me, or I'll call the police!"

By this time I wouldn't have cared had she called the whole United States Army. This woman was in the thrall of Satan, and I had to set her free. The question was how? We hadn't had any courses on casting out demons at Luther Theological Seminary.

When she stood up and pushed past me to the door, I followed her. I was so oblivious to anything except helping her that I didn't realize I was at my own bus stop. She leaped off the bus and started to run, screaming at the top of her voice, "Police! Police! Police!" When a squad car came zooming up the street, she turned and pointed a finger at me.

Two huge policemen jumped out, grabbed me, pushed me into the front seat of their car, and sat down on either side. I couldn't believe it was happening. What could I tell them? *While preaching on the bus, I saw that this woman was full of demons and I was just casting the mout?* I spoke very slowly, trying to appear calm and self-possessed. "I am a minister. This woman has fallen away from God, and I am trying to get her to come back."

"Come on now," the officer on my right sneered. "What did you really want? A woman?"

I reached into my pocket. "Here's the key to Calvary Episcopal Church House where I live. If you'll drive me there, I'll show you I'm a minister." The officer behind the wheel snorted, "Sorry, sonny; you'll have to walk home. We're parked in front of it."

The whole thing was such a nightmare that I hadn't realized till then where I was. Convinced by the key, they finally let me go. I went up to my room, dropped my clothes on a chair, too shaken to hang them up, and fell into bed, knowing beyond a doubt that what had just happened had been the worst experience of my life.

The next morning I was still in such anguish I feigned sleep so my roommate wouldn't speak to me. It didn't work. "Harald, did you hear that woman screaming for the police last night? I wonder who was after her?"

"Who knows?" I murmured, my eyes still closed.

After he had gone, I sat on the edge of the bed and buried my head in my hands. "Jesus, You know I wanted to be led by Your Spirit, but look what's come of it—just terrible embarrassment. I could have ended up in jail, my career ruined."

The Lord dealt with me in a tender way that morning, to show me that if I was going to be an instrument in His hands, I would be up against not just flesh and blood, but Satan himself. He had given me this glimpse of who the real enemy was so that I might see my desperate need of His power. I wasn't sure how I would find His power or how I would connect up to it when I did find it, but that night's experience made me realize I'd better start looking. Determined, I set out to find it.

# 2

Determination, or perhaps stubbornness, ever since I was a boy, was my most outstanding virtue and at the same time my most troublesome companion. I remember a day back in Bricelyn, Minnesota, in the spring of 1930 when I was 12 years old. I was too short and too stocky to run with the ball, but in our little town where football was the main sport, I was determined to play.

As usual, my brother Norman, who was 14, had been the first one chosen for the team. As usual, I had been the last. Norman was tall and good-looking, and whenever we played football, the girls stood on the side and cheered for him. I was tired of always being last, and this particular day I was determined that they'd cheer for me instead.

We played for over an hour, and never once did anyone pass the ball to me. It's impossible to be a football hero without a ball, and so in desperation I swallowed my pride and asked Norman to try to pass it my way. He laughed and made a face that said, "Why would *you* want the ball?" But he agreed.

We ran the play, and suddenly, to my astonishment, I was in the clear, and the ball was spiraling toward me. This was it. All I had to do was catch it and run for a touchdown. I held out my hands, and it slid neatly into my arms. I heard one of the girls on the sidelines yell, "OOH, look!"

I snuck a quick look to see which girl it was, and as I did, my feet got so tangled I splattered face-first in the mud. The ball went flying into the air, and I lifted my head just in time to see Norman catch it and run for a touchdown, to the squeals and cheers of his delighted fans.

I got to my feet and headed for home, too humiliated and furious for words. I heard Norman calling, "Hey, Harald, wait for me." But I was too angry to wait. With every step I took, I vowed, "Next time I'll show them. Next time they'll see. Next time I'll make the touchdown myself."

I was still seething when the manse with its big ivy-covered front porch came into sight. It was a square two-story house crowned with twin dormers that must have been like every other Midwestern parsonage in the early twenties. Even though I hated being the preacher's kid, it didn't seem strange to be living in a house provided by the church. It was our way of life.

Inside the kitchen, a fire was going in the stove. Mother stood over it stirring the fløte grøt, her delicious Norwegian cream gruel. My father, a Norwegian Lutheran minister like his father and uncle before him, was standing in the middle of the floor reading a letter to her. I always thought my father was terribly handsome. His deep-set blue gray eyes and strong features were so striking that they more than offset his receding hairline. He always stood erect, appearing taller than his five foot eight.

When I came in, Dad looked up. "Harald, I've got good news for you. I have just received a call to Glenwood Lutheran Church just outside of Decorah, Iowa." He paused and gave me a meaningful look. "Our new home will be only eight miles from Luther College."

Already angered from the football game, I found his good news just the excuse I needed to explode.

"Luther College! You needn't think I'm going there!" And with all the illogic of a 12-year-old, I added, "Or Luther Seminary, or into the Lutheran ministry. It's bad enough being a minister's son without becoming a minister!"

Dad didn't seem to sense how desperate I felt. "Someday you will know how fortunate you are. I was proud to be a minister's son, and as for Luther College, I spent the best years of my life there. What's more, your cousins, your uncle, your grandfather, and your eight granduncles all went there."

"I'm still not going there, and I'm not going into the ministry either."

"As much as it would please me to see you enter the ministry, that's something *you* must decide. But when it comes to your college, *I* decide."

"Dad, I'll be happy to get out of this town, but I don't want to go to Luther College, ever."

I don't know where the conversation would have gone if Mother, plump, soft-spoken, and ever the champion of her younger son, had not intervened. "Well, Harald, college is a long way off. Don't worry about it now. You have your high school to think of next."

We moved to Glenwood, but from then on, the subject of the ministry was assiduously avoided whenever I was around. At Decorah High School, I was good at studies, but once again Norman was equally good, and he was the sports hero whom all the girls admired. After he brought down a fleeing convict with a flying tackle, he was the hero of the entire state.

He spent his summers working his way around the world on a tramp steamer and sending home long, exciting accounts of his experiences, which were published in the local paper.

For four years I walked in his shadow, not nearly as tall, handsome, or successful with the girls; and in football, I couldn't even make the squad.

After graduation, I tried everything to get out of going to Luther College, but my father's will proved even more stubborn than mine. There I was again in Norman's shadow. And not only his shadow, but the shadow of all my relatives who had ever gone or taught there, including my great-grandfather, whose bronze bust looked down on me whenever I went to the library.

I had entered Luther halfway through the semester because of an operation. While everyone seemed to know everyone else, people seldom spoke to me. When they did, I found it difficult to answer. I yearned to be as at ease with my fellow students as they were with each other. Outside my room, there was a constant banter going on that I could never seem to be a part of. I dated, but only with girls whom I could be sure would accept me. Not the ones I really liked.

One day, right after the Christmas holidays, I was trudging across the campus on the way to the library when I heard someone call, "Hey, wait up." Behind me was the most beautiful girl I had ever seen.

She was wearing a red furry coat, and her soft golden hair flowed from beneath her hat as she ran toward me. On her face was a smile that just melted my heart. "Are you Harald Bredesen?"

At that instant, the power of speech departed me. But I didn't miss it. I was busy drowning in the sparkling pools of her eyes.

I nodded dumbly.

"I'm Louise Salveson, and I wondered if you would do me a favor."

I would have done anything—write her term paper, steal the king's jewels—all she had to do was name it.

"Would you give this little note to your brother? He's so dreamy, I'm afraid to talk to him."

Stricken, I held out my hand.

From then on, I stayed in my room—the one place I felt safe—and studied. I worked harder than I had ever worked before so that I would have an excuse not to have to talk to anyone. One morning I woke up with a high fever, so limp and weak I couldn't get out of bed. The dean and Norman both came to my room, and I heard them saying, "Poor Harald. He entered college late, and now he's overworking to catch up." Norman never guessed that I was sick because walking in his tall, handsome shadow was the most painful thing in the world for his short, ordinary, younger brother.

I hadn't been able to keep out of Luther College, but I knew one thing for sure: I would keep out of the ministry. After spending all my life in a provincial setting under the firm hand of my father, I longed for the romance of far-off places and the freedom of being my own boss. Being a bookworm had paid off; I had placed highest in the overall achievement tests and felt sure that I would be able to pass the exams that would lead me into the glamorous world of diplomatic service. What's more, my Congressman uncle, Harold Knutson, had promised me a good post.

Even though little was said, I knew my father was still hoping that somehow I would change my mind and follow him into the ministry. I hated to remind him that I had definitely made up my mind, and so I kept putting it off—until Christmas vacation of my junior year. We were working together in the haymow of our parsonage farm. I was on the upper level, throwing down hay for my father to pitch out to the sheep.

"Dad," I shouted, "I've decided what I'm going to do with my life!"

He plunged his fork into the hay and paused to look up at me.

"What's your decision, son?"

"I'm going to be a diplomat."

"Easier said than done."

"Uncle Harold is going to help me."

"You've decided for sure?"

"Yes."

He stabbed the hay with his fork, but his voice was resigned. "If that's what you want, Harald, I won't try to influence you." Then he spoke more quietly, as if I weren't there. "What a shame. I've always seen him as a minister."

I went back to college and threw myself into plans and preparations; my study of languages, political science, and history intensified. The moments I wasn't studying, I spent daydreaming, seeing myself in a key position in the exotic country to which I'd been assigned, with native leaders crowding to talk to me, because despite my high position, I was warm and approachable.

I envisioned a picture of myself in the Decorah *Public Opinion*, the caption telling of my great exploits, and my father looking at it with justifiable pride. The dream carried me through junior year and most of senior year.

Dad seemed to resign himself to the fact that I wasn't going to be a minister, but once when I was home for the weekend and about to leave the kitchen table after dinner, he reached over, poured me a second cup of coffee, and said, "Stay a moment, son; I want to talk to you."

He poured himself a second cup and then leaned back and ignored it. He cleared his throat. "Tell me, Harald, when you rejected the Lutheran ministry, did you reject God as well?"

So that was what was bothering him. "No, Dad, God is very real to me, too real."

"What do you mean?"

"I always feel as if He's pointing a finger of condemnation at me."

"But do you love Him, son?"

I knew my answer would hurt, but I also sensed that I had to be absolutely honest. "No, Dad. I can't say

I love Him. I feel as much love for God as a debtor does toward his creditor when he has reneged on his debt."

"I see. But you do believe in Him."

"Yes, I believe in Him. And I respect Him. But I avoid Him."

"Yet you still go to church?"

I met his eyes. "Yes, Dad, out of loyalty to you—besides, it's the easiest place of all to shut Him out."

My father got up from the table and stood there, polishing his glasses. "Well. Thank you for being honest." Then he turned and left the room.

Actually, my life was so busy there wasn't time to think much about God at all. The whole world of diplomatic service was beckoning to me, and stronger than ever. Letters between Uncle Harold and me flew back and forth full of suggestions, hopes and plans.

Norman, who had graduated and was now in Flight School, came by the college and stopped in my room. (It was the spring of 1940 and all Europe was at war.)

"I hear you're going to be a diplomat, Harald. That's great! It's a field I'd never make it in, but I know you're going to be a success." I was thrilled. For once in my life, I was walking in my own limelight.

It was nearly the end of my last year when I went home as usual for the weekend. On that Sunday I awakened to a world sodden with rain, and I went to church only because I couldn't come up with an excuse for staying home.

I walked slowly up to the old stone church and into the back, looking around for a pretty girl to sit next to, and finding none, chose a seat in the last pew, where I might assume a prayerful attitude and take a nap. As the old hand-pumped organ wheezed out the last minor strains of the pulpit hymn, my father ascended the wooden steps of the high pulpit and there, under the ornate Victorian canopy, adjusted his glasses and announced his text, as he had done a hundred times before. He recounted for us the events following the death of Christ when He appeared on the shores of Galilee and asked Peter, who had denied Him, a single question: "Simon, son of Jonas, lovest thou Me more than these?" When my father repeated Christ's question a second time, "Simon, son of Jonas, lovest thou Me?" something happened to me. I sat up in the pew, my dreariness vanished. I felt electrified.

Once more my father slowly repeated the words: "Simon, son of Jonas, lovest thou Me?" As he spoke, the pulpit, the pews—everything—just disappeared, and a Jesus totally different from the one I knew stepped out of His Word, and I saw Him for the first time. I can't explain what happened, but in that moment, no one else existed for me. It was just the two of us. He was speaking to me, only to me. "Harald, lovest thou Me?" There was no pointing finger, only outstretched arms.

I started to say, "No, You have just made me uncomfortable," but I could not finish the sentence. It was no longer true. I no longer felt uncomfortable, just exactly the opposite. Instead of condemnation, I felt total acceptance. I was overwhelmed by His love for me and by my love for Him. I was beginning to see who He really was. Wow! All my plans and ambitions for my life fell aside. So *this* was Jesus—so lovely, so loving, so loveable. "Yes, Lord! I do love You more than these, more than myself, more than anything." In that moment I had but one desire: to give joy to the heart of Jesus.

I wanted to run right up to Dad in his pulpit, put my arms around him, and tell him what had happened, but I managed to wait until the service was over. As soon as he chanted the benediction and turned to go into the sacristy, I dashed down the side aisle in order to get there before anyone else did.

He was putting away his vestments, and his back was toward me.

"Dad?"

"Yes, Harald?"

"Dad, while you were preaching, something happened to me ... I—I can't put it into words. Everything's changed."

"What's changed, son?"

"When you preached on Peter, Jesus became real to me. I didn't even hear you, Dad. I just heard Jesus, and do you know what He asked me? 'Harald, lovest thou Me?'"

My father turned slowly around and looked at me. "And how did you answer?"

"I said, 'Yes, Lord.' Then He said, 'Feed My sheep.' He was calling me to be a minister, and that's what I want to be. That's what I've *got* to be. I can't think of anything more exciting, more wonderful."

"Harald!" His face was beaming. He put his arm around my shoulder. Then it dropped, and he turned quickly back to the vestments, but I had already seen the tears sliding down his cheeks.

With great joy, I reversed my plans, and the following September entered Luther Theological Seminary in St. Paul, Minnesota.

Even now I hate to admit this, but because of my experience that Sunday morning in Glenwood Lutheran Church, I entered seminary feeling my call to the ministry was more special than that of my fellow seminarians. I felt I was one of the very few Jesus had ever spoken to in such a real way. Since I knew how God acted—He worked in very Lutheran ways, through very predictable Lutheran means—I decided that with me, He had just stepped out of His predictable pattern for a moment. It was something He didn't go around doing for just anybody.

I thought this way until one day close to the end of my second year at seminary. I was hitchhiking along St. Paul's Fort Snelling Parkway. Home was still 165 miles away when a large black sedan stopped to give me a lift. The driver was a young man, about 32 and somewhat on the gaunt side. His plain dark suit and slickedback hair made him look so severe that when he offered me his hand, I thought, "Oh boy, what am I letting myself in for?"

"My name's Morno," he said.

It was a name I'd heard before, but I couldn't place it. As we headed into the canyon road, I suddenly remembered: Morno was the name of a notorious mobster of the Twin Cities area, now in the state penitentiary.

We rode in silence for a while as I looked again at the slim man with the slick hair. Slowly, apprehension filled me as I realized that the man I thought was safely behind bars was, in fact, sitting next to me.

I gulped and asked, "You're the head of the Morno gang, aren't you?"

He turned and smiled, a surprising, beautiful smile. "Ex-head. Praise God!"

His warmth and amazing exclamation broke the tension in the car. I said, in a voice that I knew must have been incredulous, "You're a *Christian?*"

"Sure am!" The way he said it made being a Christian sound exciting.

A half hour later and 20 miles down the road, he was still telling me his story. "I was dying. I had chronic nephritis, and the prison doctor had leveled with me. I knew I had little time left. I tried not to let on how scared I was. I just lay there thinking. The person who kept coming to my mind was Grandma. I thought of the time she came home and told us she had gotten saved, and the change we saw in her. From then on it seemed like I could never talk to her but she would come out with something about the Lord—her 'Jesus kick,' I called it. Finally I got real mad and told her to shut up. She did—she never spoke another word to me. But many times I saw her come out of her room with red eyes, and I always knew she had been praying for me.

"There on my cot, it was the words she spoke to me when I was still a teenager that kept on coming back to me. 'I see the way you're going, Warnie, and I can't stop you. You're running away from God, but one of these days you'll come to the end of your rope. When you do, cry out to Him. No matter how hopeless you feel, cry out to Him!'

"Before I knew it, I was crying out, 'Jesus, Jesus, save me!'"

Then Warren told me something that seemed impossible to believe, and yet I found myself believing it.

"I was lifted—it must have been three feet or more—and suspended a moment above my bed. I felt the power of God go through my whole body. I heard a voice. It was not just mental. It was a real voice. Just my name and three words, 'Warren, you are healed.' When I was lowered onto my bed, I knew that I was. I was a changed man. I could hardly believe I was me.

Everything, everyone, looked different. All my friends, all my enemies ... I just couldn't get enough of the Bible. Every spare moment I had, I was reading it or praying or trying to talk to someone about Jesus. Now I'm out on parole—living for Jesus."

As he talked, I felt like the disciples on the way to Emmaus. This man knew Jesus in a way that I had never dreamed of knowing Him. Even more than his story was what I sensed in him. I had never seen anyone burn so for Christ. He was like a flame, and my own heart burned within me when I talked to him.

Then he turned to me and said, "Now tell me your story."

Tell him *my* story? Up to that moment, I had thought I had a story to tell. Sure, Jesus had come to me just as really as he had come to Warren. The big difference was, that to Warren, He was even more real now than at the time of their meeting.

I shook my head and replied, "I love Jesus, too, and I know Him," but before I could say, "but not like you do. How do I get to know Him like that?" he was slowing down to let me off. "Well, here is where I turn. How about a word of prayer before you get out?"

Watching his car gather speed, I knew that whatever it was that Warren had, I wanted. But I had no idea where to find it.

# 3

I can still hear the rich bass voice of my seminary roommate, Joe Belgum. "To one empty head, add four years of college, two years of theology, one year of internship, one more year of theology—" He stopped and grinned. He could see I was depressed, and he thought his recipe for a half-baked Lutheran minister might give me a laugh. I tried to grin back, just enough to show my appreciation for his effort, but not enough to encourage him to go on.

Tall, blond and handsomely rawboned, Joe, like me, was the son of a Norwegian Lutheran minister. But here the similarity ended. My boyhood had been a sheltered one; Joe's had not. While still in grade school, he had had to go to work; he could hardly remember a time when he had not held down a job of some sort to help support, not only himself, but also his family. In the rough and tumble of the work-a-day world, he had developed an exuberant confidence in God and his own God-given abilities.

I could understand his confidence in himself, but what I could not understand was his confidence in me. He seemed to think that I could do anything—be anything. I could not understand it, but I loved it, and I loved him for it. On this day, however, my confidence was at a low ebb. It was 1943, and America was bursting with war workers and patriotic slogans. Here at seminary, Joe and I were facing the biggest challenge yet—our internship, a year to learn by doing, under the watchful eyes of an experienced pastor. Each of us would be assigned a parish and a pastor to work under for a year. Then after one more year at seminary, we would be ordained, and I would become a naval chaplain.

It was a chance to prove our mettle or lack of it. Our strengths and weaknesses would be duly recorded and reported to Dr. Gullickson, president of our seminary. He, in turn, would share them with the faculty, with us, and with future call committees.

"Maybe you're looking forward to this year, Joe," I told him, "but I'm not. Our whole future hinges on how well we do, and I'm scared. In the right parish, under the right man, sure. But supposing I get assigned to some old curmudgeon with whom I can't have real fellowship, the kind of guy who would see the worst in me instead of the best? You know, a guy like Pastor H."

Joe had been tilted back in an old office chair, his feet on the desk. He swung himself around, planted his feet on the floor, and faced me. "Harald, you've been seeking God ever since you started seminary. He's not going to let you down now."

Suddenly it dawned on me that Joe was right, and I started to laugh. "Of course He's going to look out for me! He's probably already picked out just the right man for me, probably chose him for me before the foundation of the world, and here I'm worrying about it." Now we were both laughing.

Joe stood up, put his hand on my shoulder, and began to pray. "Father, put Harald under a man who really knows You, a man with whom he can have close fellowship, who will challenge him to go deeper with You."

After Joe's prayer, my worries evaporated. There are many warm evangelical pastors in the Lutheran ministry, and I was confident that God had chosen one of them for me.

I arrived at my new assignment, Bethlehem Lutheran in Aberdeen, South Dakota, with high spirits. But before my first week was out, I knew with Job that the thing I feared most had come upon me. God had answered Joe's prayer by putting me under John Dahl,[1] the most coldly intellectual man, it seemed to me, in the entire Lutheran church. We had theological and philosophical discussions, but absolutely no fellowship. Not only did he never talk with me about Jesus, but he seemed upset when I talked with others about Him.

I can still remember that painful moment when I started sharing the Lord

---

[1] Names have been changed here and wherever necessary to permit candor without embarrassment.

with a hungry-hearted young couple and looked up to see Pastor Dahl glaring down at us. In a voice trembling with anger, he rasped, "Is he trying to ram that stuff down your throats, too?"

As time went on, I became more and more convinced that the only thing we had in common was our mutual disappointment in each other.

I wanted desperately to tell someone how difficult life was, but the number-one requirement of an intern was that he be loyal to his superior. Our instruction sheet had made it abundantly clear: "My superior, right or wrong, my superior." My lips were sealed. But a little seven-year-old girl's were not. Coming out of church one morning, I heard her say, "Mommy, I wish Pastor Dahl wouldn't talk so much about pillospy." I wanted to hug her. I wanted to say, "Out of the mouths of babes and sucklings..." but I didn't let on I had heard.

Most of our members, however, seemed well satisfied with "pillospy." That is, until a physical or spiritual crisis came into their lives. Then they looked elsewhere. Some of them turned to a brash young Assemblies of God minister, a Pastor P.G. Emmett, who had taken to the airwaves to declare, "Not only does Jesus still save, He heals and fills with the Holy Ghost." To prove it, he put people before the microphone to testify to healings that most of our members lumped as "incredible!" That is, until they themselves got hopelessly ill.

Then some of them were willing to take a second look. They went over to his "tabernacle"—and they never came back. According to Pastor Dahl, they had fallen victim to a form of religious insanity. For the victims he had pity. For their "victimizer," vitriolic scorn. "I bumped into Emmett on the street," he told me one day. "He came up to me and stuck out his hand, but of course I ignored him. I hope he got the point."

Though our pastor ignored him, more and more of our people did not. He was beginning to make a dent on our attendance. Even in a church of 1,600 members, we couldn't go on ignoring continued inroads on our membership. One morning Pastor Dahl came into my little office with a thick pack of cards. They were the names and addresses of straying Lutherans. "Look these people up," he said, "and see what you can do with them. I want a written report on each one."

The first family on my list was the Gunnar Ericksons, one of the less prosperous families in our flock. Although the senior Ericksons had never been too regular in their church attendance, we had sorely missed their three lively youngsters in our Sunday school. Peter, the youngest, shouted my arrival: "Mommy, Mommy! Pastor Bredesen's here!" Peter had stopped coming to Sunday school, but apparently he was still my friend. I found "Mommy" bending over a washboard, but she smiled when she saw me, wiped her hands, and shook mine.

I told her that we had missed them in church for the past couple of months. She smiled half-apologetically. "Well, we've missed being there—the children have especially. But we could never go back. As members, I mean."

Then she told me why. "When our little Peter was dying of pneumonia, Dr. Johnson and Pastor Dahl prepared me for the worst, but I was not willing to accept it. I couldn't believe it was God's will for him to die. Even though I'd been warned against Pastor Emmett, I sent for him. As he was praying, Peter coughed up something that had been lodged in his lungs. In no time at all, he was his rugged little self again." As she spoke, my eyes followed her gaze through the window to the yard outside where Peter was trying to roll down a little knoll with a puppy in his arms. Seeing the radiance in his mother's face, I could not find it within myself to urge her to come back.

With the second "victim," I fared no better. She was a woman in her fifties. "I had a large external goiter," she said. "It was the painful kind. I was due for an operation. And then one morning I happened to hear Pastor Emmett's broadcast. He was saying that God didn't have anything against doctors. They were His gift. He healed with them, without them, and if necessary, in spite of them. The problem is, he said, that most Christians take their case to the doctor first and to God last, when it should be the other way around. Right on the air, he asked, 'Are you due for an operation? Before you have it, why not try Dr. Jesus?'

"It just seemed he was talking to me. That night, I sneaked over to his church. After his sermon, Pastor Emmett and his elders prayed for me, and then they said, 'Claim your healing, sister.' I didn't feel anything, but in the taxicab on the way home I coughed up my goiter into my handbag. I've been fine ever since. Praise God!"

This woman I found much much harder to believe, and yet I could not wholly doubt her, either. Unable to make up my mind, I shared her account with a medical friend. She laughed and said, "That's impossible. That wasn't her goiter she coughed up, but her calciferous deposit." Whatever it was, what had been diagnosed as a goiter was gone.

The next stray I did not have to go see. When I called him on the phone to make an appointment, he said, "Don't bother to come to see me, Reverend. On my day off, I work for Pepsi Cola, and tomorrow morning I service your vending machine."

The next morning I went to my office 20 minutes early, and as I walked up to the church door, there was the Pepsi truck parked alongside. *Some eager beaver,* I thought. *He must be anxious to talk.* He was. A reddish-haired young man of about average height and weight, he had nothing outstanding about him, except his eyes. They were about the brightest blue I'd ever seen.

"It was my eyes," he began, "that were my problem. They were so crossed that without very thick lenses I was practically blind.

"My doctor told me that the only solution would be an operation, a very delicate one that might not be successful. Just the same, I decided to go ahead with it. But meanwhile we started slipping over on Sunday nights to Pastor Emmett's church. One night I went up for prayer and half a dozen people laid hands on me and prayed real hard. Afterward they told me, 'Now you must take your healing by faith. We prayed that God would heal you, so believe that He has and act accordingly.' Someone asked me,

'Suppose you knew that God had healed your eyes, what would you do?' 'Why, I guess I'd throw away my glasses.' 'All right, do it.'

"I did. But many times afterward I wondered if I had done right. My eyes were as bad as ever. The guys on my section gang are a pretty rough lot. And they didn't spare me. When they asked me what had happened to my glasses, I told them. What made it hard was that without my glasses I was as blind as ever. And when they saw me staggering and stumbling all over the place, claiming to be healed, they razzed me unmercifully. They kept on and on. They were always playing practical jokes on me. All this time I tried to make myself believe that God was just testing my faith and that my healing would manifest itself any day, but six weeks went by and still no healing. Brother, was I discouraged!

"One morning I went down into our basement prayer room and cried out to God until I didn't have any voice left. Nothing happened. Finally, exhausted, I started groping up the stairs with my hand on the rail. Then suddenly everything came into sharp focus. Right on that stairway, Jesus had touched me."

As I looked into his eyes, so straight and clear, it was impossible to believe that they had ever been otherwise, or that they were the eyes of a man who would tell a lie. This is what shook me the most. These people just weren't the kind to tell lies. What if they were telling the truth? The possibility fascinated and, at the same time, appalled me. I knew that if they were telling the truth, it would open a whole new dimension of Christian life and experience to me. I knew that it was going to cost me something to find out, possibly even my future in the Lutheran ministry. I also knew there was only one thing more costly than accepting a new truth, and that was rejecting it. But did I have to do either? Couldn't I just sort of table the whole thing until I'd established myself in some secure ministerial post?

Then, as I was reading the book of Revelation, 14:4 leapt out at me: "These are they that follow the Lamb whithersoever he goeth." It was as if the words were written in light. I knew that, through them, God was speaking to me. And He was saying, "The Lamb is Jesus, and Jesus is Truth. Are you willing to follow Truth, wherever He leads you?" Not since that rainy Sunday morning in Glenwood Lutheran Church had I been asked a question upon which so much depended. I felt like a man jumping off a cliff, but I found myself saying, "Yes, Lord."

The day after I heard the story of the crossed eyes made straight, I went to see a parishioner on our sick-call list, a Mrs. John Burkhart, who, at 47 years of age, was confined to her wheelchair by an exceedingly painful kind of arthritis. Over the course of 18 years, she had become almost completely immobilized. As I sat and talked with her, the thought came to me: *Why don't you ask God to heal her?*

I answered myself, *Harald, don't be ridiculous.*

*But,* I countered, *He healed those others.*

I batted it back and forth and left her home without mentioning a word about it. While walking back to the rectory, I couldn't put it out of my mind. Finally I decided, "If God heals today, if the three people I talked to were honest, if Warren Morno was telling the truth, then this is where I find out. I'm going back there tomorrow and tell her God will heal her."

The rest of the way home, my spirit soared at the thought. But during the stiff evening meal in Pastor Dahl's dark-paneled dining room, the possibility of God healing today seemed less and less real. I wondered, *Suppose she prays for a healing, and God doesn't heal her? What will happen to her then? Will it destroy her faith? At least now she has faith. Maybe I should leave well enough alone.*

As soon as dinner was over, I did something most people would consider awfully naive. I took a Bible off the top shelf of the church library and, with my eyes closed, let it fall open of its own accord.

"God, if You heal today, show me in Your Word."

When I opened my eyes, my finger was on Psalm 103:3: "Bless the Lord, O my soul, and forget not all his benefits: *Who forgiveth all thine iniquities; who healeth all thy diseases."*

That was all I needed. The next morning, I went to Mrs. Burkhart, and as I told her all that I had heard and what had happened, I could see hope lighting up her face. Then together we claimed James 5:14: "Is any sick among you? Let him call for the elders of the church and let them pray over him, anointing him with oil in the name of the Lord. And the prayer of faith shall save the sick, and the Lord shall raise him up, and if he has committed sins they shall be forgiven him."

Before I prayed for her, I called Mrs. Burkhart's attention to verse 16, which says, "Confess your faults one to another and pray for one another that ye may be healed."

I reminded her that arthritis is often caused by negative emotions, and that there was no use praying over the symptoms unless we dealt with the cause.

"Is there anyone toward whom you cherish resentment?"

"Oh, no, I love everybody!"

"Everybody?"

"Why, yes, everybody."

I don't know what possessed me, but I persisted.

"Everybody?"

She started to say for the third time, "Everybody," but paused. Then after several moments, she replied, "Well ... my brother ... he beat me out of a will. I could never love him."

When I tried to show her the cost of her unforgiveness, of which her 18 years of suffering was just the first installment, she replied, "Yes, I know everything you say is true, but after what he did, I just could not love him ever again."

"Of course not; you have no love to love him with," I told her, "but are you willing to ask God to love him through you?"

"Why yes," she said, looking quite relieved. "That I could do."

So she did, and then we asked God to heal her. I think she thought I fully expected God to do it. But as I uncorked the little bottle of oil I had brought in obedience to Scripture, and made the sign of the cross on her forehead, my faith was so weak I felt as if I was just going through motions. I could not believe that God was going to perform a miracle for us. I had so very little faith—just barely enough to obey. But, praise God, that is all that He asks. I was to learn from this experience, not to ask God to increase my faith, but simply to help me to act on the faith I already have.

The next day, I went back to see how she was. During the night, my faith curve had sagged even further; it was now down to the 2 percent expectancy, 98 percent resignation mark. To my amazement, she welcomed me with a radiant smile.

"Pastor! Last night, for the first time in 18 years, I had absolutely no pain!"

And almost before I realized it, Mrs. Burkhart was out of her chair, taking care of her family as a mother should. After that I did go to a service at Pastor Emmett's church, and despite the tremendous difference between it and our own liturgical worship, at first I did not feel too uncomfortable.

Then suddenly, everyone began praying at once. Their voices rose louder and louder. Some were weeping, some appeared to be laughing, and I was actually frightened. *These people are working themselves into a frenzy,* I thought. *What would happen if they all should turn on me?* I felt like a duck out of water and surrounded by wolves. I stuck it out to the end of the service but never went back. And it wasn't just my reaction to the noise that kept me away, but the fear that word would get back to Pastor Dahl and through him to my professors. I didn't know how I would explain to our seminary president what I was doing in an Assemblies of God church.

Even though I didn't return to the church, I did return repeatedly to the homes of the people I had met, and there I found the warm, loving fellowship I so desperately craved. Finally, the internship was over, and I was back at seminary for the last year. Joe was consoling me. "Too bad about your assignment. I thought sure God would answer our prayer for someone with whom you could have real fellowship."

I stopped unpacking and thought a moment. "You know, God did answer that prayer. It wasn't the way we had expected, but He heard my heart cry for Christian fellowship. He gave me such remarkable friends that this past year was more than I could ever have dreamed of."

I couldn't tell Joe, because I didn't see it myself for many years, but there was another reason why God put me under an icy intellectual so early in my ministry. His coldness forced me to look outside the circle to which I would otherwise have confined myself. Had God given me what I had asked for—a cozy church and a warmhearted pastor, I never would have discovered that the Lord is doing the same things today that He did 2,000 years ago. Perfect Father that He is, He doesn't always answer the literal verbiage of our prayer, but the substance of our heart cry.

# 4

Graduation was around the corner. Although I had prayed for the naval chaplaincy, I had not passed the physical. While Joe and I were sorting out our books and personal belongings, we speculated on the future. Most of our class had already received calls. Neither of us had.

"The right place for me will come along," Joe said with his usual confidence.

I had always lacked his assurance. "Well, I wish I knew where I was going. My father is coming up here for graduation, and the first thing he'll ask is, 'Where have you been called?'"

Joe shoved books into a crate. "Tell him the truth, that you don't know yet."

"It's not that easy."

"What do you mean? You'll get called. Everyone does. Does it matter to you where God sends you, as long as you know it's Him doing the sending?"

"Well, quite frankly, Joe, it does matter. Terribly. Sure, I want God's will.

Ever since He called me, I've wanted it, but that doesn't mean that I'm not scared of it. I want to be a success, someone my parents can be proud of. They've always wanted the very best for me. For my sake and—let's face it—for the family's sake as well. In our family, success means so much, perhaps too much. But what if God wants me to be a failure—in the world's eyes, I mean, or even in my parents' eyes? Do you think that could be possible, Joe?"

He sat down on the crate and looked at me. "That's a funny thing, Harald, that you should talk about success and failure at the same time."

"Why?"

"Because this morning at breakfast I heard a few of the guys discussing you." He started laughing. "They said you'd either be the biggest flop or the biggest success this seminary has ever had."

So he thought that was funny! He would! He had so much confidence that he didn't care what people said, but I thought of all the times I *had* flopped—football, girls, projects that never got off the ground. Even though

I knew I could be a colossal failure, it hurt that my classmates felt that I could.

The thought that I might wind up the seminary's biggest success seemed so farfetched that I pushed it out of my mind. Almost, but not completely. It was right at that time that I saw a religious classic, *The King of Kings.* It was technically outdated, but still very powerful. Before it ended, I hatched what I thought was a brilliant scheme. Why not make a really great new film of the life of Christ?

I discussed it with Joe. "We'd use the finest technical resources available and enlist the greatest artists in the world. With the war still on, we'd call it a sacrifice of thanksgiving for world peace." I talked it and dreamed it for days. I lay in bed at night and planned it aloud, with Joe across the room commenting on it in the dark.

"Can't you just picture the splendor of it? It would be a religious film to end all religious films. All the great communions of the world would be represented. We'd have the Resurrection music of the Greek Orthodox, the

Passion music of the Lutheran. There would be the Gregorian chant and Negro spirituals. They say *The King of Kings* has already grossed eight million; we could make far more than that and give it to a worthy cause." I paused for breath. "What do you think so far, Joe?"

The answer from the next bed should have been a warning. Joe's single commentary was, "Z-z-z-z-z."

Undaunted, the next week, using stationery from the campus bookstore with the seminary letterhead on it, I sent out a prospectus to the 40 top religious leaders of the day, telling them the plans for this great new movie—who the stars would be and how it would be done. Then I asked each of them to be on the sponsoring committee.

The man I was most eager to enlist was Dr. John Sutherland Bonnell, pastor of New York's Fifth Avenue Presbyterian Church and author of our text on pastoral counseling, a course that Dr. Gullickson himself taught. Dr. Gullickson had an almost awed respect for Dr. Bonnell, and much of it had rubbed off on me. With such a wealthy and influential church behind him, imagine what a man like Bonnell could do. I sent him a letter. "If you had eight million dollars, how would you use it?... Prospectus follows."

Inevitably, rumors of my project reached Dr. Gullickson, and I was called to his office. This would be my second visit to that inner sanctum. The first had been eight months earlier, the painful occasion when Dr. Gullickson had informed me of the contents of Pastor Dahl's scathing report on my internship.

This morning I found him sitting behind his desk, a large, wavy-haired, floridly handsome man of the old school. He was usually solemn, and today he was stern-faced and stern-voiced.

"What's this I hear about you sending letters out to some of my colleagues? And on seminary letterhead?"

There was nothing to do but explain. I shared my vision for a fantastic motion picture to unite the Christian faiths of the world. When I was through, he leaned across the desk and fixed me with his eyes. "Young man, I have two fears for this project: one is that it won't succeed; the other is that it will. My advice to you is: Take the feathers out of the wings of your visionariness and put them in the tail of your good judgment."

"But, sir, I've already heard from Dr. Bonnell. Would you like to hear his telegram?" Dr. Gullickson nodded, still the picture of the indignant president.

I pulled the telegram out of my pocket and read, "Am much interested in your exciting proposal. Meet me 5P.M. Wednesday, LaSalle Hotel, Chicago."

Dr. Gullickson's eyebrows shot up, and his mouth quivered with surprise. He cleared his throat. "Hmh." Then his manner changed. "When you see Dr. Bonnell, ask him if he can come here to address our convocation. I've written him three letters, and he's not answered any of them."

I left his office overjoyed. In the back of my mind there was a wisp of a voice that seemed to be saying, "You're not even ordained, and already you're a success."

Dr. Bonnell was in the lobby of the LaSalle, which turned out to be the most elegant hotel I had ever seen. I assumed I would wait for him, but there he was, standing tall and straight, looking every bit as aristocratic as the church he pastored. He was waiting for *me!* I realized anew what an important project I had actually dreamed up.

He took me by the arm and hustled me to his room, as if he couldn't get me there fast enough. He closed the door and blurted, "Now tell me about the eight million dollars!"

"Didn't you get my prospectus?"

"Prospectus?"

"The plan for how the money can be earned."

"You mean that you don't *have* eight million dollars?"

"Why, no." All of a sudden I was scared. Dr. Bonnell's face turned red, and he struck the table with his hand. "Young man! Do you mean you've wasted my entire afternoon on a half-baked scheme?"

I stood there speechless, not believing what I was seeing and hearing. He walked across the room and leaned hard on the dresser. "How *dare* you write me such a brazen letter and ask how I'd use eight million dollars when you don't even *have* eight million dollars!"

I was so crushed I could have cried. The "biggest success" had become the "biggest flop." Didn't he know that I had been as excited about getting his support as he had been about the money? Then with bewildering suddenness, he slapped his knee and burst out laughing. He guffawed. I stared at him. How could someone change from such outrage to hilarious laughter?

He said, "You know, this project is probably going to succeed! It's visionary, but so are most churchmen, and if you can get enough visionaries to see the same vision, it'll become a reality." He was all encouragement.

We talked for almost half an hour, during which he shared how he had hoped to help returning GI's with the eight million dollars. I completely forgot to ask him to speak at convocation.

When I got back to the seminary, there were five more replies waiting for me, all of them positive. One was from the president of Princeton Seminary, Dr.

John MacKay, accepting membership on my steering committee. Another acceptance was from Dr. John R. Mott, founder of The World Alliance of the YMCA and the International Missionary Council, whom *Time* had dubbed "the greatest layman of our day": "I'm happy to be on the sponsoring committee of this most worthy undertaking.... The project is of such importance, you must come to New York to guide it."

As I read his words, excitement raced through my body. Here it was. My call. I, Harald Bredesen, newly ordained Lutheran minister, would be going off to New York to produce a film so marvelous it would unite the religious world. How was *that* for success?

When my parents came for the ordination, Dad asked, "Have you received a call, Harald?"

"Yes, Dad. I'm going to New York."

"Wonderful." His eyes lit up. "What church?"

"No church, Dad. I'm going to make a fantastic motion picture of the life of Christ."

"You're not going into the ministry?"

"It's a different kind." And I told him what had happened.

"It doesn't sound like any kind of ministry to me." Then, half relenting, he put his arm around my shoulder and sighed, "Well, it's your life." But the light in his eyes was gone.

# 5

The sun had already set that June Saturday in 1944 when the train finally pulled into New York's cavernous Grand Central Station. The lady behind the information counter didn't smile when I asked her for directions to Sloane House, YMCA. "Take the IRT to 34th, westbound crosstown bus to 9th."

*Not very sociable,* I thought, but I was too excited to mind. Here I was at last, in the biggest, most important city in the world. The dark subway train I caught seemed filled with intrigue, and I sat on the edge of my seat, looking at the people around me. Where were they going? Where had they come from? Wouldn't it be great to talk to every one of them?

The thrill of being in New York was still with me as I checked into my room at the Y. I asked for the cheapest room and got it. It was small and musty smelling, only big enough for a cot, wardrobe, table and chair. The window looked down on the post office truck depot. But neither smallness, nor smell, nor view mattered. I wouldn't be there long. There were people to see, things to do, places to go.

My first meal was in a luncheonette down the street. Sitting on a stool, I ordered a hamburger and milk. Beside me was a young woman I would have loved to have talked to, but what did one say to a woman in New York? Besides, I was afraid my Iowa accent would make me sound like a hick, for it seemed to me that every person I had met so far had a sophisticated city way of speaking.

When the hamburger came, it was delicious. Everything about New York seemed delicious to me that first day. I decided that I would write a long letter home and tell the folks about it before the time came when I would be too busy to write long letters.

Monday morning I went to Dr. Mott's office in the sedately impressive Presbyterian Building and outlined my idea. He was delighted. "You know this is the kind of thing that the World Sunday School Association should get behind. They have member councils in 57 countries. I'll give you a letter of introduction to the general secretary, Dr. Forest L. Knapp." As I took the elevator up to Dr. Knapp's office on the twelfth floor, I felt as if I was scaling Mount Olympus. I sat in the reception room waiting for him, visualizing how thrilled he would be with my project that had been labeled so visionary. When his secretary ushered me into his office, he stood up to greet me, a tall, erect man with a noble forehead and blue eyes that beamed out at me through sparkling clear glasses. He looked every inch the Christian statesman I was prepared to meet. His genial warmth and obvious interest in my project convinced me that I had gained his support.

A few days later, he called me into his office, where he sat behind a huge mahogany desk. He motioned me to a chair. "I'll get right to the point: I see no future for your project."

"Wh-what?"

"I'm sorry. It's just not feasible."

"But what about all the people who've said they'd back it?"

"They're backing it in name only. Where would you get the money? How would you organize such a thing when you don't even own a motion picture studio? What makes you think the finest actors in the world would invest their time in a film produced by amateurs?"

"But we'd get professional producers. And there are men right here in this building who would give their time."

"No, Harald. It's far too complex for such a simple solution. Besides, there are more important things to be done with our man hours."

"But ... it would unite the religious leaders of the world."

"Would it? It might divide them, especially if it fails."

"The answer is no?"

"The answer is no."

My head swirled and my stomach felt like I was dropping 20 floors in a runaway elevator. If Dr. Knapp turned it down, no one would ever touch it. I thought of my father. *"It doesn't sound likea ministry to me."*

Then I was struck by another thought: What would I do in New York without the film to work on? I had no friends, no other reason to be here. Norman had sent me a one-way ticket, and I didn't even have the money to get home. While Mount Olympus came crashing down around me, Dr. Knapp continued, "Even though we're not interested in your project, Harald, we *are* interested in you. Anyone who could spark so much enthusiasm for such a hare-brained scheme as this has a real gift for promotion, and we would like to have you on our team. How would you like to be the public relations secretary for the World Sunday School Association?"

When I accepted his offer, my only emotion was relief.

That night I sat down and wrote a letter to my father.

Dear Dad,

You were right. The motion picture idea was visionary, but let me tell you the wonderful new ministry that has opened to me...

Despite my glowing letter home, my work with the World Sunday School Association (which by now was calling itself the World Council of Christian Education) was not enough to keep out the loneliness I was beginning to feel in New York. Every day when I left the office, I entered a world that was as indifferent to me as my classmates had been those first few months at college.

I was riding home on the subway when it came to me that there was not one thing intriguing about a subway. It was dark and dismal, and the thousands and thousands of people that it transported were as cold and closed to conversation as the mannequins in the window of Macy's.

My room at the Y was not a prison cell, because I could leave it whenever I wanted. But those hours I spent inside it were as lonely as a cell must be. I knew every crack in the plaster and every cobweb on the ceiling. The musty smell whenever I came in was thick and sickening, and there was not even anyone to complain to about it. I dared not write too many letters home. After I had gone to Coney Island, to the top of the Empire State Building, and taken the Staten Island ferry, there was really nothing left to say, and I was afraid the utter loneliness of my life would somehow creep into my words—and my parents would guess that New York City had conquered me before I had had a chance to conquer it.

At night I walked with heavy feet into the luncheonette that served delicious hamburgers; only the hamburgers were greasy, and I wondered how I had ever thought them anything else. I sat on a stool, and the counterman half smiled and said, "Hi." I knew it was that half smile and one friendly word that brought me back over and over. Next to me, an older woman was eating a tuna sandwich. "Pardon me, but do you have the time?"

"Eight-fifteen," she said with a half-filled mouth, and kept right on eating.

When she left, a man took her stool, and I asked him the time, too.

"Eight-twenty-five." Like the lady before him, he offered no more. Didn't anyone guess or care that I asked the time just to hear the sound of another's voice? Sometimes just to hear the sound of my own voice? Around me, people were talking to others in the clipped funny twang that was the hallmark of New Yorkers. How could I have ever thought it sophisticated? How

I longed for the slow-paced Norwegian accent of the good people of Glenwood, Iowa!

One night, I found a friend, an old friend, one to whom I could talk to about everything. I was sitting in my room leafing through my Bible when my eyes fell on the words of Jesus. "Simon Peter, lovest thou Me?"

I remembered my answer that day in Dad's church. "Yes, Lord, I do love You," and I said the words now out loud. For a moment the tiny room with its drab cot and scarred furniture seemed to glow as I realized that all the while I had been looking for a friend, I already had one.

Gradually, Jesus became my meat night and day. I became totally dependent on Him and tried to keep Him continually in my thoughts. Day by day His presence became more real and constant. One night I was reading C.S. Lewis's *Beyond Personality*. When I read that God knows what He intends to make of us, and He never gives up on us, I found myself holding my breath like a man reading a mystery thriller. I thought, *Imagine being so caught up in something spiritual. Something must be happening to me.*

Because I always woke up early, I had several hours to read the Word and pray and to memorize a dozen lines or more of some old Lutheran hymn whose words and melody would run through my mind all day long. I worked hard at practicing the presence of God.

In my office there was a clock that Norman had rescued from a torpedoed ship. Every quarter-hour the bell would strike, and I would stop and read a Bible verse and pray for another name on my prayer list. One day, walking down the street, I found myself saying the name of Jesus, over and over again. He had become so sweet to me in my loneliness that I wondered again what was happening to me.

Gradually my work at the World Council grew more interesting. My job was simple enough. I was there to enlist sponsors who would help us raise money. Dr. Knapp briefed me my first day on the job: "Now that the war is ending, the Council is about to launch a great reconstruction project. Since many of our 57 national member councils are in the European and Asian theaters, we are out to help each of them restore the Christian education systems of their countries. This will take great sums of money. To acquire this money, we must have names on our sponsors' list so big that they will attract other men of wealth and influence and at the same time impress the man in the street with the significance of this project."

My marching orders: Enlist as sponsor everybody who is anybody.

I was thrilled by my assignment. The money we were raising was Jesus' provision for evangelizing the children of the world. I set out with enthusiasm.

I wondered, *Who's big in our country? Whose name is so impressive that other people will want to join us if he's a part of our organization?* I thought of Vice President Truman and went to Washington to try to get an appointment to see him. On the phone I told my story to a secretary, how the World Council of Christian Education needed Truman to be a sponsor for our European postwar reconstruction project, and I would like an appointment to see him. She said, "Just a moment."

Click-click-click. Then I told my story to someone else. Then another click-click-click, and I told my story again. Click-click-click, and I repeated it the fourth time. Finally I heard a cheery voice say, "This is Harry Truman. What can I do for you?" I could hardly get my breath. Here I was, a green country boy, talking to the vice president of the United States.

I choked the words out: "The World Council of Christian Education is launching this great postwar reconstruction project, and we'd like to use your name as sponsor of our Waldorf-Astoria Kick-Off Dinner. Madame Chiang Kai-shek is our vice president. Dean Weigle of Yale Divinity School is our chairman, and Crown Princess Marta of Norway will be our guest of honor at the dinner."

Truman answered, "Why, certainly."

"Well, thanks."

He hung up.

With the phone still in my hand, I suddenly remembered that what I really wanted was for him to be sponsor of the overall project itself, not just to attend a dinner. How could I call him back and have him think I was so stupid I forgot what I called for in the first place? My whole body began perspiring as I stood with the dead receiver in my hand. This was my first venture forth, and I was determined. Besides, this project was crucial to the evangelization of the children of the world, so once again I went through all the waits and the clicks, got ahold of him again, and made my second request. Once more he agreed.

Shortly after that, bold headlines proclaimed: ROOSEVELT DEAD. TRUMAN PRESIDENT. Was I glad I made that second call!

Now with the president of the United States as a sponsor, we easily signed up leaders around the nation who let us use their names: Herbert Hoover, Mrs. Calvin Coolidge, Henry Ford, Harvey Firestone, Jr., and on and on. Across America, small and great, rich and poor saw the names that were supporting the World Council of Christian Education, reached into their pockets, and gave generously to our fund.

As it turned out, even more important than having the president of the United States behind us was the glamor and appeal of Captain Eddie Rickenbacker, who was also a trophy of that Washington trip. Having been a flying ace in World War I, he had risen to even greater heights during World War II, and at this particular moment was the number-one hero, it seemed, of nearly every American. Over his name, and on his personal stationery, we sent out five hundred thousand *highly* personal letters of appeal and hundreds of telegrams.

My father called one day on Dr. Tinglestad, a Luther College professor friend, and found him exuberant. "Guess who I just heard from," he glowed. "Captain Eddie Rickenbacker! Look, a personal letter, and I didn't even know he knew me."

In her next letter to me, Mother recounted what happened: "Your father took the letter and read it aloud—

Dear Dr. Tinglestad,

You were lost—

A child alone, forlorn, do you remember what you felt—the panic

that twinged at your stomach, the grief that quivered at your mouth—
You wanted to be brave but—but—
Then a hand on your shoulder, a gentle familiar hand, and you weren't lost anymore.
That, Dr. Tinglestad, is the story—
"He stopped, folded the letter, put it in the envelope, and handed it back to Dr. Tinglestad, 'My boy wrote that.'"

Dr. Tinglestad blew his stack, and the World Council of Christian Education was out one contribution that would have been ours if Dad hadn't spilled the beans. But others made up for it. That one letter alone sent the number of contributors skyrocketing, by 900 percent. We all rejoiced, but for different reasons. The rest of the staff rejoiced because they really believed in the work the Council was doing and were confident that the benefits would eventually filter down to the little children of the world. I had believed that, too, but after six months, I could no longer overlook the fact that the Council was not actually centered in

Jesus Christ. God had obviously put me there to make it so, just as it had started out to be back in the 1870s, when John Wannamaker, H.J. Heinz and other devout Christians had founded it.

The more successful I was in raising money, I reasoned, the more quickly I could carry out my scheme. I yearned to see this money actually being used to bring a living, personal Jesus to children around the world and had convinced myself that the end justified the means. So, while others worked to strengthen the Council, I labored to get into a position of sufficient leverage to transform it.

Actually, I was already successful. At least I thought I was. Everybody who was anybody, it seemed, was now behind us. The only group that didn't sponsor us was royalty. There was not one crowned head on that whole, long sponsors' list. Dr. Knapp and I did a lot of brainstorming on that one, and we finally came up with the answer: a summons to the world, especially prepared for their Royal Highnesses' signatures. It would be a regal proclamation, reminding good men everywhere that we must begin now to lay the spiritual foundations of world peace in the hearts of little children. I went down to Washington and got the president's signature. Since we already had him as sponsor, and since these were the days of Lend-Lease largess, it was easy to get King George VI, King Haakon, King Gustave, King Christian, Queen Wilhelmina, and Generalissimo Chiang Kai-shek to join him in signing this world-shaking document. Never in the annals of public relations had royalty been so cooperative. I was beginning to see that big people will lend their names to anything that bigger people are connected with; that, as the Bible says, people *are* like sheep—the bigger the people, the more like sheep.

Here we were, in a little old office on the twelfth floor of the Presbyterian Building in New York City, cooking up an idea that could make the king of England take pen in hand and summon the world. We had persuaded four kings, a queen, and two presidents to sign the same document. That was better than the medieval popes could do.

More and more I saw myself as a master chess player. The world was my board, and real kings and queens were my pawns. The loneliness of my life didn't matter, because something else had become obvious. I was a success.

"Thank You, Jesus, thank You, thank You." And I wrote home still another glowing report, reminding my parents that I was in touch with leaders all over the world, and here I was, only 26. As the picture unfolded, it became more apparent to me why God had put me in this strategic position. In my euphoria, I could see that He was going to give me control of the purse strings of the World Council. Then I would be able to put Bible-believing evangelicals in key positions. We would take over the Council, and through its 57 member councils, reach the world for Christ. This was God's master plan of evangelism. I marveled at His wisdom.

My primary assignment, to enlist sponsors and, through them, contributors, was being crowned with success, but a secondary responsibility remained: cultivation. "Properly cultivated," an expert told me, "the average donor will not only repeat his gift, but increase it year after year. The secret is to find dramatic new ways to convince him that the money he gives is actually getting to the field."

What, I wondered, would be a "dramatic new way"? Suddenly I had it. I almost ran to the office of Dr. Chester Maio, our Chinese National Secretary. I knew I must work quickly. Within a week, he would be returning to Canton.

Two months later, Mrs. Gilmore, a blue-eyed, snowy-haired dowager, marched triumphantly into the office. "This will *thrill* you!" She handed me a long, narrow, sky blue envelope printed in red Chinese characters and postmarked "Canton, China."

Carefully, I extracted the letter from the open end. The stationery on which it was written was coarse and brown. It looked almost like paper toweling, it was so rough, but the letter was beautiful. It was a heartwarming, very personal thank-you, to Mrs. Gilmore from our Chinese National Secretary in Canton, in appreciation of her invaluable help to the Christian teachers of war-torn China.

"It came in this morning's mail," she said. "I knew you would be interested."

I was.

That coarse brown stationery, that looked almost like paper toweling, was paper toweling. I had purchased it in New York and sent it to Chinatown to be imprinted and multigraphed, then shipped to China, and from Canton, mailed to our American donors—an indirect approach, but cheaper, believe it or not, than sending our cultivation letters in the regular way. Cheaper and so much more effective.

Mrs. Gilmore was beaming. "It's so nice to know our gifts are getting out to where the need is."

At Christmas, during a flare-up of Jewish-Arab hostilities, a prosperous middle-aged couple dropped in at our office. "We just received a Christmas greeting from Bethlehem," the wife explained. "Not Bethlehem, Pennsylvania, mind you—Bethlehem, Palestine! It's from the General Secretary of your Palestine Council."

"What does he say?" I asked.

"It's a thank-you letter. It's so beautiful. It's ... it's like a poem. Here, I'll read it aloud." Half-cooing, she read:

From Bethlehem, whose hills first heard the angels sing, we send you Christmas greetings.

You know the strife that makes this land run red with blood and blaze with hate—

Yet midst the shouts of fighting men, the song of angels still is sung by children.

Those who taught them, *you* helped train ... Arab, Jew, Armenian...

She paused to dab her eyes. "Isn't that beautiful!"

I wanted to say, "Glad you like my stuff." I didn't. Nor did I tell her that the card had come even farther than from Bethlehem to New York—twice as far, to be exact. It had been printed in Brooklyn.

Her husband looked hesitant. She nudged him, "Go ahead, dear, tell him."

Half-sheepishly, he confessed. "I have an apology to make. I've been telling my wife that she was foolish to keep on giving so much money to a big, sprawling council like yours, because probably not one dollar in a hundred would actually get to the firing line. Glad to see I was wrong. Please accept my apology."

We did.

The little blue paper he pressed into my hand as he went out the door helped. It was a check to the Council for 500 dollars.

Then came a letter of appreciation written in pencil. Of the hundreds of letters on that pile, I just happened to pick it up. As I read it, I wished I hadn't.

Dear Captain Rickenbacker,

Thank you for your wonderful, wonderful letter. My husband and I have been praying for you for years, but never did we expect to hear from you. When your plane went down in the South Pacific and they couldn't find you, we prayed for you. And when they were ready to give up the search, we kept on praying. How we rejoiced when they found you safe on your life raft! We were so thrilled the way you told how you and your men had prayed, and God had sent a sea gull and those flying fish to feed you when you were starving, and how He sent the rain when you were dying of thirst. What a testimony to the world that our God is a great God, a living God, a loving God.

Oh, how I love Him. I'm so glad you love Him, too, and that you want the children of the world to know Him. My husband is too sick to work, so we are on relief, but when we got your letter, we wanted so much to help that we skipped two meals to send you the enclosed dollar. It's such a small sacrifice, but we hope it will help some lost little child to find his way to Jesus. God bless you, Captain Rickenbacker, and all those wonderful, wonderful people who are helping you in this great cause.

In the precious name of Jesus,
Emma Cartwright


I could not bear to stay in the office. I hurried downstairs and out into the pouring rain. In a matter of minutes, my coat and shirt were drenched and cold. Yet the stinging rain against my face felt good, like something I deserved. Stubbornly I clung to the idea I was serving Jesus at the World Council as over and over again I tried to reason it all out. "I haven't said one word that isn't true. I'm not deceiving anybody. I am serving Jesus. I have to do what I have to do."

But I walked on, letting the torrents wash over me, like water over the hands of Pilate.

# 6

It was a week later that Dr. Knapp decided that it might be better for me if I were to move out of the Y into a place that would, as he said, "broaden me." Back in my little room, I took the three dresser drawers and dumped their contents on the bed. Then I began stuffing all my worldly belongings into a suitcase, a cardboard box, and two shopping bags. I was grateful to be moving, grateful to be doing anything that would take my mind off my work at the World Council. Yet as I packed, the conversation I'd had the day before with Dr. Knapp kept running through my mind.

He was one of the finest men I had ever known, but it had occurred to me that I had never heard him speak of his own relationship to Jesus Christ. I had gone into his office and blurted, "Dr. Knapp, do you believe that Jesus Christ is God?"

He replied, "Certainly there was more of God in Him than in any other man." He gave me a smile and returned his attention to the papers on his desk.

"Well, I believe He is God."

Dr. Knapp looked up and spoke without a trace of impatience. He was never impatient. "You must remember, Harald, you come from a very constricted parochial Lutheran background. And that's the only point of view you've ever been exposed to."

"That's the only one I care to be exposed to."

"I see, but don't forget you're working with a global ecumenical organization. You should at least become aware of the positions of other denominations, what they believe, and why they believe them."

I couldn't disagree. Except for that brief encounter with Pentecostals in Aberdeen, I didn't know very much about anything except Lutheranism; nor, up to that point, had I felt the need to.

Dr. Knapp continued. "Just to broaden you a little, Harald, I'm going to suggest that you move into Calvary Episcopal Church House. It's nearly as evangelical as yourself, but at least it's ecumenically oriented, and I think it would do you good to live there."

So I was packing my clothes, getting ready to become broadened. I knew I would never change my beliefs, but it wouldn't hurt to find out what others believed. My new home, Calvary Episcopal Church House, was a slightly Gothic, 12-story, red-brick parish center adjoining Calvary Episcopal Church.

The two buildings looked out on historic Gramercy Park, a square block of wooded greenness, flanked by four-story, whiteshuttered brick townhouses dating back to the early 1800s. Protecting the park from the public was a high wrought-iron fence and a massive iron gate. Before I lived there, it had always been to me a symbol of smug exclusiveness, but during my two-years' stay, this "exclusiveness" became "privacy," a privacy to cry out to God undisturbed, something I would have great need of.

Dr. Knapp's hope that Calvary House would broaden me was more than realized; my stay there changed the direction of my life. Moreover, it happened far more quickly and abruptly than either Dr. Knapp or I could have imagined. God's instrument was Dr. Samuel Shoemaker, the rector of the church.

Though he was to become most famous as the founder of the "Pittsburgh Experiment" (you would try a new razor blade for 30 days, why not try Jesus for a similar period?), he had already launched Faith at Work Fellowship for businessmen and was at the height of his career, writing books, addressing vast radio audiences, and pastoring. Because of Dr. Shoemaker's unusual gift of discernment, coupled with great love and a willingness to speak truth under all circumstances, God had frequently used him as a shepherd to bring straying sheep back into the fold. A fact I was not aware of at the time, but was about to discover.

After dinner that very first night, Dr. Shoemaker invited me to join him by the fireplace. I was deeply honored. Here was a man who was not only a famous churchman, but also a real soldier of Jesus Christ!

We were in the cozy second-floor meeting room and I was relishing the setting. The low hand-hewn beams, leaded windows, and medieval art gave it the feeling of an old English castle. Dr. Shoemaker smiled at me, sank back into his deep leather chair, and said, "Now tell me about your work at the World Council."

I scarcely knew where to begin. "Well, I suppose you would like to know how I got President Truman as our sponsor ... Next was Eddie Rickenbacker. After I had landed him, our contributions jumped 1,100 percent. And through him I was able to reach Henry Ford, Herbert Hoover, and Mrs. Calvin Coolidge. I guess you already know about Queen Wilhelmina, King George VI, King Christian..."

After about an hour, I paused to give him a chance to express his astonishment. I expected him to say, as everyone else did, "How in the world did you do all that?"

He leaned forward in his chair, any suggestion of a smile gone, and looked me straight in the eye. My own smile faded as the silence between us grew longer. When he finally spoke, it was with an awesome authority. "What exactly are you doing for these men spiritually?"

I felt as if I had been kicked in the pit of my stomach. I couldn't breathe.

"Are you leading them to Jesus? Or are you just using their money, names and influence? If you are exploiting them, you will explode them."

I literally gasped for air. Eventually I gained a semblance of composure, but I had no words to answer him with. He waited calmly, never taking his eyes from mine. At length, I stood up, shook his hand, and left the room.

From that moment on, I could no longer convince myself that my motives in the World Council were strictly evangelical. Night after sleepless night, I'd steal out into the privacy of Gramercy Park. The big creaky gate would open to me a small silent world, the one place I felt free to pace back and forth and pour out my heart to God. I loved the sound of that gate clanking closed behind me. It shut out the world, and it shut me in with God. I paced back and forth, scuffling the dry leaves before me in the darkness, clearing a path. As I walked, I prayed, I groaned, I cried. I agonized aloud, letting my thoughts run over and over.

"Am I exploiting the great men I contact? Am I deceiving the little people our promotion reaches? Oh, Jesus, am I really doing what You want? Or have I been rationalizing Your will instead of seeking it?" The words of Joe Belgum at the seminary would repeat themselves over and over: "either the biggest flop or the biggest success this seminary has ever had." "I'm not a flop. I haven't failed. Please, Jesus, don't let me fail. But am I trying to succeed just to be a success? Am I doing what You want? I don't know."

Then I'd think of Dad: "It doesn't sound like a ministry to me." "Maybe it's not a ministry, but it's the only thing I know how to do." I spent one entire Friday evening begging God to show me.

The following morning, as I was buttoning the collar of my shirt, it became so tight I felt I would strangle. I knew I couldn't face another day. I prayed, crying out, "Oh, Jesus. I can't go on this way, half for myself and half for You. I'll split apart." I got down on my knees and begged. "Jesus, do with me what You want. Put me to digging ditches in North Dakota or working in a state insane asylum. Just so I'm sure I'm where You want me, doing what You want me to do."

I stood up then, confident beyond all reason. I *knew* that Jesus had heard and would lead me where He wanted. Maybe it was the World Council. Maybe it was somewhere else. But one thing I knew for sure: It was out of my hands and in His.

That night I kept a routine appointment and found myself in the McAlpin Hotel talking with a man named Abraham Vereide. He was the founder of International Christian Leadership and the man responsible for the Presidential Prayer Breakfasts, where the president and some 1,600 of the nation's leaders gather each year to hear the gospel. I had come to know "Abram," as we called him, when I was making contacts in Washington, D.C. He had given his help, not because he believed in what I was doing, but because, for some reason I could never figure out, he seemed to believe in me.

Through his work, he had met and influenced many world leaders for Christ. On that night, he sat in the corner of this very ordinary hotel room, a ruggedly built, commanding figure, with chiseled Nordic features, smiling blue eyes, and distinguished gray hair, telling an extraordinary story. It was how he had gone to the Netherlands when Prince Bernhard was about to divorce Queen Juliana for being a religious fanatic. He led the prince to Christ, and the royal family was restored.

He said, "When you reach a leader for Christ, you reach not only him, but also those who follow him." He stood up and walked across the room to me. "Harald, this is what you should be doing. The men whose money, names and influence you have been using, you should be leading to Christ. I'm getting on in years, and I believe God would have me hand my mantle over to you. You could start off as my assistant."

His words shook me to the core of my being. Right there in front of Abram

Vereide I fell on my knees and cried out, "Lord, this morning I handed my life over to You, and now I've received this call to reach these men for Christ. I'm almost certain this call is from You, but I must be absolutely sure; if it is, please confirm it in three ways: Make yourself real to me, more real than You've ever been before, lead me like a child, and open the doors. If You do, I'll go to anyone and tell them about You."

It was at midnight that I shook hands with Vereide and left his room. So much had happened that my head was whirling. Fifteen minutes later I was walking along 34th Street alongside the Empire State Building. As I walked, I saw myself as I really was, all the pretensions stripped away. I said, "Lord, how can You ever use me to reach leaders? I'm vain, selfish, self-seeking; I'm proud, and I'm not really honest. I'm double-minded, immature, unstable, scatterbrained, thoughtless, forgetful. I do crazy things without thinking first." I shook my head as I walked along.

Then, like the gong of a bell, came the words: "God has chosen the foolish things of this world to confound the wise." I cried out, "Yes, Lord! On that basis, I qualify."

God had made it so simple that my heart filled with gratitude. I wanted to get down on my knees, at half-past midnight in the middle of New York, and thank Him. A little song of praise and gratitude welled up through my lips, nothing I'd ever heard or sung before. Just then I became aware that a man was walking alongside me. His face was so shining that it seemed I could have measured the light with a meter. He said, "You're a Christian, aren't you?"

"Yes."

"As I came up behind you, the Holy Spirit said to me, *'I have need of that man. Speak to him.'*"

"Well, who are you?"

"My name is John Gounaris, and I'm from Glad Tidings Tabernacle. I'm sort of God's minuteman. I go wherever He sends me, like Philip in the book of Acts."

For some reason, his saying all that, standing there in the middle of the night on the sidewalk, didn't seem at all incredible. I said, "Well, maybe He did send you. This morning I handed my life over to God, and just a few minutes ago He called me to reach world leaders. I was just asking the Lord how He could ever use me." "He will use you.

But first you must let Him empower you as He did His apostles."

"What do you mean?"

"Look at the Bible," he told me. "Look at Acts 1:4-5. You remember how before Jesus ascended into heaven, He instructed His apostles to wait in Jerusalem until they were baptized in the Holy Spirit?"

"Yes. We call it Pentecost; it's one of the four great festivals of the church year.

"Yes, and that's just it: We make it a festival, when the apostles made it an experience. Stop and think a moment: What happened then? The apostles were filled with the Holy Spirit and began to speak with new tongues. From then on, these men who had been so cowardly became bold as lions. Remember how Peter stood up and addressed that great crowd—the same

Peter who had cowered before a servant girl? What had changed him? It was the Holy Spirit." Then John Gounaris put his hand on my shoulder. "And how do you think you will reach leaders? It will be through the Holy Spirit. He will empower you. He will equip you. He will open doors for you that no man could open."

I drank in every word he spoke, knowing that God had sent him to me this night as surely as He had sent me to Abram Vereide earlier.

"How do I get this power?"

"Ask Jesus to baptize you in the Holy Spirit."

"But where in the Bible does it say He will do this?"

"Reread the Gospels. In every one, Jesus is introduced as the one who will baptize with the Holy Spirit. Today, all over the world, people are receiving Him as their Baptizer."

I could hardly believe what I was hearing. I had gone through seminary, and yet I'd never realized before that we are to appropriate Jesus as our Baptizer just as definitely as we appropriate Him as our Savior.

John continued, "Don't you remember the prophecy from Joel that Peter quoted that first Pentecost? 'I will pour out of my Spirit on all flesh.' That's what's happening now. Men are receiving the Holy Spirit and speaking with new tongues. Miracles are happening. People are being healed."

*People are being healed.* All of a sudden I thought of Pastor Emmett's church. People *were* healed there. There *was* power.

As much as I wanted to embrace all he said, I held back. It was so unorthodox, so un-Lutheran, that I didn't know what to say. John seemed to sense how overwhelmed I was. Once again he put his hand on my shoulder. "Come to Glad Tidings Tabernacle tomorrow afternoon and seek this for yourself."

It was two in the morning when we finally parted. I climbed aboard the bus and sat down. And that's when I heard the Lord's voice say, *Preach to the people on this bus.*

That was the night, of course, when I was humiliated beyond words—the night when God showed me beyond a shadow of a doubt that if I was going to reach leaders, I would be up against, not flesh and blood, but the devil himself. After that experience, I knew I needed to receive the Holy Spirit. My heart was filled with anticipation the next day as I set off for the afternoon service at John Gounaris's church.

# 7

Formerly a synagogue, Glad Tidings was a fairly large old church in downtown Manhattan. There were about 400 people waiting for the service to begin. Most of them gave the appearance of being working people. Yet in contrast to some cold, upper-class churches filled with fashionably dressed people, there was a sense of joyous expectancy such as I had never felt in a church before. At the end of the service, the minister said, "If any of you here have a deep sense of need, come forward to this altar."

I wanted to go, but the church was so different; I didn't know what to expect. I didn't see a soul there I knew. My sense of need, however, was so great, I made myself step out and take that long walk down the aisle to the front. I was halfway down when I saw him, Vernon Huffe, my old high school buddy. There he was, standing behind the altar, as tall, gangling, and open-faced as the last time we had played nibblestick together in his backyard. He stood there grinning at me, every bit as surprised and delighted as I was. He reached out his hand, and I grasped it, completely reassured.

Vernon said, "Since I knew you, Harald, the Lord has saved me and filled me with His Spirit. Now I'm a chaplain in the Navy." As I told him about what had happened the day before, he smiled even more broadly. "That accounts for the unusual events that led me here this afternoon. Now I *know* that God has sent me here to meet you at this altar."

It seemed I had a thousand questions to ask. Vernon started to answer them and then stopped. "Harald, why don't you take a couple of weeks off and come to our camp meeting in Green Lane, Pennsylvania? You'd meet people there who would have time to answer your questions and pray with you. You could really seek God."

"Sounds like a good idea." But the words were hardly out of my mouth before I began to think, *I can't go off to a Pentecostal camp. What would Dr.*

*Knapp say, or for that matter, any of my friends.*

As I was going out the door, an old woman came up to me and said, "I'm so glad to see you here. You don't know me; my name is Emma Fowler, and I heard you speak over at Christian Soldiers Mission. Yesterday morning while I was doing my housework, this tremendous burden of prayer came over me. It was so great that I could hardly stand up under it. I had to get down on my knees and cry out for you, in groanings and tears and tongues. I said, 'Lord, what is the meaning of this? I need prayer worse than he does!' The Lord revealed to me that you were at the crossroads of your life. I prayed to God then that you would make the right decision."

I was so moved to hear that a stranger had been down on her knees in prayer for me the very moment that I had turned my life over to God that I went back to Vernon and said, "Tell me again, how do I get to this camp?"

A week later, I was there. The Lord had timed my vacation just right so that I could spend it at Green

Lane—"seeking God," as Vernon had called it.

As a vacation spot, Green Lane Camp left much to be desired. The "Tabernacle," looking like a big, open-sided warehouse, sat on the edge of a wooded slope, bordering a hilltop field. In the wooded area below were tiny cabins, connected by winding paths. I was given a mattress tick, told to fill it with straw, and then take it to a cabin where I would be sleeping on the floor along with eight other fellows for the next week or so.

What Green Lane lacked in physical comfort, it more than made up for in spiritual opportunities, and it was for these that everyone, some 350, had come. They assembled twice during the day and again in the evening for the preaching and worship services. I could actually feel their love for God, for each other, and even for me. I knew that these people were closer to the first-century Christians than any people I had ever met. I couldn't get over how at peace they were, and how they loved one another. So *this* is what Christianity was meant to be!

For the first time, I heard messages in tongues. During the service, someone would speak out in a foreign language unknown to himself, I discovered, or to anyone else in the congregation. Then he or another person would be given the interpretation and speak it out as a message from God. I'd studied linguistics when I was preparing for the diplomatic service, and I knew the difference between articulate speech and gibberish. This was articulate speech.

Most impressive of all was a sense of the presence of God such as I had never known before. It was everywhere. I almost expected to look up and see the Pillar of Cloud that hovered over the camp of Israel in the wilderness.

There was just one thing that I considered odd. Finally I had to ask about it. I turned to the man next to me and said, "Why do you raise your hands when you pray?"

He grinned. "You'll find out."

My favorite place to pray was in a long low shed with plain wooden benches and a straw-covered floor, just behind the speakers' platform of the tabernacle.

I'd go there until long after midnight, seeking the face of God and letting Him search my heart for any area of unsur render or disobedience. One night I was down on my knees in the straw, kneeling with my face in my hands. Throughout the place, people were praying out loud in little groups or by themselves. I lifted my eyes and looked around, and as I did, I thought of the warning of Oswald Chambers, in my favorite devotional book: "All-night prayer meetings can be a positive snare. It's dangerous to open yourself too wide. The wrong spirit may come in."

All of a sudden I stood up, frightened with this horrible picture of myself as a howling demoniac. In my mind's eye I could see my father standing there in the prayer room, watching me and saying, "Harald, my boy, you have gone off the deep end, and now you are too far gone to realize it."

Suddenly, the straw-covered room seemed ludicrous, and so did my search for the Holy Spirit.

# 8

The next day I couldn't even pray, I was so afraid. Then I made myself turn to God. He spoke to me through Luke 11:10-13: "If a son shall ask bread ... of a father, will he give him a stone? Or if he ask a fish, will he for a fish give him a serpent?... How much more shall your Heavenly Father give the Holy Spirit to them that ask Him?"

What a relief those words were! I got down on my knees again, knowing that if I asked God for the Holy Spirit, He wasn't going to give me a serpent.

For 10 nights I prayed. Old men and women and little children would come up and pray with me and encourage me. Each night I grew wearier than the night before. I tried to pray the words of the liturgy: "Blessed art Thou. Holy art Thou. Worthy art Thou." As I grew more tired each night, they became just words with no meaning. On the tenth night, I was so weary I could think of nothing else. My body seemed to have no strength. My eyelids seemed to be weighted shut. Even my bones seemed like they could no longer stand one on top of the other. I thought, *Oh, the luxury of a bed. What a wonderful thing a bed is! Wouldn't it be marvelous to belying back in bed, stretching out and going to sleep?* I looked around, and here were all these people wanting to help me, seeking so earnestly for me. For once, my stubbornness was a boon. I turned to the Lord and said, "If it gives You any satisfaction, if it gives You any joy, I will praise You until I drop." I abandoned any thought of going to bed. And in that moment, I was invaded by the Holy Spirit. I jerked awake as He began to give me a glimpse of Jesus' worthiness. How utterly worthy He was of glory. What a tremendous price He had paid for our salvation!

It was just as if this salvation He had wrought for us was a great reservoir of sparkling, pure water. Over on the other side was a huge, parched wilderness—unfruitful, unproductive, barren of life. It seemed as if this water was yearning to burst its dikes and pour out over that desert to beautify and fructify it. But there was one bottleneck, and that was Harald Bredesen. Not my sins; I had repented of all of them. It was my desire to serve God only on my own terms, being unwilling to die to myself. That was keeping the Salvation of Christ, which He had wrought at such price, from pouring out through my life into other lives. In that moment I abhorred myself, and I said, "Oh, Jesus, make me after Thine own heart." Jesus seemed so close, I felt as if I could touch Him.

In the midst of this, I heard a woman shouting in my ear, spraying saliva on me as she yelled, "Throw your hands up, throw your hands up! You'll never get the Holy Ghost that way!"

Abruptly, I was filled with loathing. The nerve of her, intruding on my moment with Jesus! Then, the incongruity of seeking the Spirit of Love and feeling repugnance for a woman who was only trying to help, dawned on me. I prayed, "Lord, give me Your love for that woman."

Immediately I was bathed in love for her, for God, and for everyone else, and I began to stammer, "Ab ... ab ... ab..." like a little baby learning to talk.

I thought, *These Pentecostals speak insuch clear tongues. They're going to think there is sin in my life obstructingthe flow.* But I kept on. "Aba ... aba ... aba ... papa ... Papa!... aba Papa!" and suddenly I realized what it was I was saying, something from Romans 8: "For you have not received the spirit of bondage again to fear; but you have received the Spirit of adoption, whereby we cry 'Abba, Father.'" And I began to speak other phrases with increasing fluency.

But then a disturbing thought intruded itself: *How am I ever going to interpret this experience to my professors at Luther Theological Seminary, to Dr. Schiotz, the president of our denomination? Maybe if I can be very analytical throughout the experience, give them a detail-by-detail account, including the psychological factors involved, they will decide that I was in full possession of my faculties and that there was no violation of my personality.*

So, while my spirit was meeting the Holy Spirit, my mind was concentrating on Harald again. I began describing

myself in scientific phrases: "How is it,"
I asked myself, "that I am speaking
these words that I have never studied?
Is it cerebral process, or is it through
nervous stimuli, or is it through direct
control of the facial muscles?"

As soon as I got my mind off the
person of Christ and on to the
phenomenon, I was left high and dry
and desolate, utterly desolate. It was
as if I had nothing, no love, no Spirit,
no Jesus—nothing.

I walked across the camp to my
cottage and crawled into bed, as
saddened and backslid as a man can
feel. I thought of the Scripture, "My
soul shall take no pleasure in him, if
he draw back." Here I was, on the
brink, and I turned back. Now God had
turned His back on me.

The next morning, I couldn't have
felt more unspiritual or unready to
receive the blessing. The man who was
speaking that morning, Pastor Arthur
Graves, said that during the war, two
men in a dive-bomber had been
descending at the fearful speed of 600
miles per hour. The canopy had blown
off their plane, and they had been

exposed to extreme pressure. Though they were able to right the plane, they stepped out of the cockpit drenched in their own blood.

"What was the problem?" he asked. "The greatness of the pressure? No," he continued, "it was not the greatness of the pressure, but the inequality of it. If the pressure on the inside of their bodies had been exactly equal to that which was on the outside, they would have escaped unscathed. You can have a billion tons of pressure on one side of a tissue-thin sheet of paper, and if there is exactly a billion tons on the other side, the paper won't even be torn." He went on, "You and I are living in a day of ever-increasing pressure. As Satan sees his time growing short, he is going to exert such pressure against the saints as the world has never seen. But God has a pressure, the infilling of the Holy Spirit, a pressure on the inside equal to every pressure that Satan can exert from the outside. So no matter what you are called upon to endure, you can come through completely unscathed."

Then there was a message in tongues spoken in great tenderness, and to another, the Holy Spirit gave an interpretation in equal tenderness that melted my heart completely. God was saying, "O my people, if you could stand where I stand and see this world hurtling toward destruction, littered with broken and wounded hearts—I long to take the healing balm of My gospel and pour it into these hearts. But to do so, I must have channels, human channels, completely yielded and surrendered to Me. Will you not yield? Oh, will you not yield?"

For the first time in my life I realized the heartbreak of God: that it was not only the sin of the sinner, but the satisfiedness of the saints, that we are satisfied with having so little of Him, and He having so little of us.

Up to this point, I had wanted power for service, power for witness, and power to live the Christian life. Now I had one desire, and that was to satisfy the yearning heart of Jesus with myself. Previously, I had loved God with reservation, had served Him with reservation, and therefore I had assumed that He loved me—with reservation. In that moment it seemed as if all my sins and repeated failures and shortcomings had no more power to shut out His love for me than a flyspeck could shut out the sun. In spite of what I was, in spite of what I was not, in spite of all my reservations, He loved me *without* reservation. I was so overwhelmed, overjoyed and amazed by the total unreservedness of His love for me that my hands went up in awe. Now I didn't have to ask anybody, "Why do you raise your hands?" It was just involuntary wonder and surrender.

I tried to say, "Thank You, Jesus, thank You, Jesus," but I couldn't express the inexpressible. Then, to my great relief, the Holy Spirit did it for me. It was just as if a bottle was uncorked, out of me poured a torrent of words in a language I had never studied before. Now everything I had ever wanted to say to God, I could say.

After a long time of praising God, and knowing that this experience was real, came the return of the realization that I was going to have to tell my friends. I knew what they would say:

"Harald, you have gotten yourself mixed up with a group of hysterical people who whip themselves up into a frenzy of religious excitement then let off steam in a form of ecstatic gibberish. All this has rubbed off on you."

I prayed, "Lord, if this is a true language, then You can reveal it to me." I went out the door and down one of the many paths that lead into the surrounding woods. As I walked along this path, my new prayer tongue was flowing, an artesian spring within me, of praise and adoration.

Coming up the path was a pretty flaxen-haired girl of about 11. When she came to me, she stood and cocked her head and laughed. "You're speaking Polish."

I wrote on a slip of paper, "Where is there a Polish man? I want to speak to him." I was afraid to start speaking in English, afraid I'd never be able to begin again in this tongue. The girl led me to a man who was standing on the front steps of his cabin; he was squat and muscular, maybe a Pennsylvania miner. I thought, *Just think, I've never met this man, but in Christ we are brothers.*

He exclaimed, "Bracia, Bracia! You call me Brother." He said, "You are praising God, going from one Slavic dialect to the other."

When I left him, my heart was overjoyed. I returned to the camp praising the Lord Jesus for baptizing me in His Spirit. The first two things I had asked God to do for me if He wanted me to reach leaders, He had done. He had made himself real to me—gloriously, unspeakably real. He had led me like a little child, step by step, and now I knew He would do the third thing. He would open the doors, and I would go through them to the world leaders He had called me to win.

The following Monday I returned to the office at the World Council. Dr. Knapp was in Europe, others were on vacation, so there were only six of us at staff devotions that morning. Though it wasn't my turn, I asked if I could lead. We sat around a table in Dr. Knapp's office. As I began my story, starting with meeting the man on the street, I could see each person's mouth drop open in total surprise. There wasn't a noise or a shuffle as I continued through to the end, and then tendered my resignation. When I was through, nobody spoke. Finally, someone said, "Harald, please wait for Dr. Knapp to return."

Somewhat reluctantly, I agreed.

# 9

There was someone else with whom I could hardly wait to share, a girl, a very special girl who had come to mean a great deal to me this last year in New York. Ever since that time in college when Louise Salveson had given me an instant's hope, before she asked me to deliver her note to Norman, I had looked for someone like her, someone as beautiful and sweet as Louise looked that day, but I couldn't seem to find her. Then one day as I was lying on the floor doing calisthenics in my room at Calvary House, the door flew open, and Ben Armstrong, who roomed across the hall, burst in with his news.

"Harald, I've found her!" He stood grinning down at me as I finished my sit-ups.

"Found whom?" I managed to grunt.

"The girl you said you were looking for—you know, one with beauty, verve, deep spirituality! This girl's got all of these, plus."

"All these, plus?" I stopped to look up at him.

"Yeah, man! Plus a pixie smile, a Georgia-peach complexion—she is from Georgia—a voice like honey, and lots of little extras."

Ben, a young seminarian doing postgraduate work at New York University, had already found the girl he had been looking for, and now he was scouting for me. "Harald, you are about to experience love at first sight."

I got off the floor. "What's her name?"

"Ever see those roadside signs, 'Hollingsworth Candies—for people who like fine things'?"

"Sure. All the way from Virginia to Florida ... don't tell me—"

"That's right, this is *Jane* Hollingsworth." And then, pleadingly, "Harald, old boy, you won't let her millions stand in the way of true love, will you? Promise?"

"I promise. Now, how can I meet her?"

"Easy as pie. Come with me to the Inter-Varsity meeting at N.Y.U. next Wednesday; she's a staff member. Then, if you like what you see, ask her for a date."

The following Wednesday I went with Ben and did indeed like what I saw. She was not tall—which was definitely in her favor as far as I was concerned. Her hair was golden brown, and her voice and skin were just as Ben had described them. But what especially attracted me were "the little extras," like a glow that made an interesting face beautiful. She had the expression of one savoring something, which filled her being with joy and laughter, and you knew immediately *Who* that something was.

At the end of the meeting I went up to her. "Jane," I said, "do you like to eat by candlelight on a scrubbed pine table in front of a crackling fire?"

"Young man," she asked with mock seriousness, "just what are you proposing?"

"I'm proposing a date. At the Washington Irving Inn. Right now! It's just a stone's throw from here."

So there we were in that tiny basement dining room, eating braised chicken livers and other colonial goodies at a scrubbed pine table, by candlelight, in front of a crackling fire. I had often imagined myself sitting at that table with that very special girl I knew God would someday bring across my path—a girl who would have all the qualities I could ever want in a wife, a girl exactly like the one who sat across the table from me now. What a beautiful spirit looked out at me through those laughing green-blue eyes! It was all I could do to keep from proposing on the spot.

Later that evening, we dropped in on a Faith at Work meeting in Irving Harris's apartment. The room was packed. As Jane and I were going out the door, a young Army doctor cupped his hands to my ear and, under cover of the hilarious leave-takings going on around us, whispered, "Harald, Jane's the one. As you came into the room together, the Lord revealed to me that you are meant for one another, you complete each other." As if I needed convincing.

I needed even less convincing after our second date. We spent the day sailing on Long Island Sound—at least, that's what our host was doing. As for Jane and me, we lolled on the deck, reveling in the hot sun and a lazy breeze that was just barely strong enough to push us up the Sound and back again. By the end of the day, we were red as beets and totally sapped of energy. That night in church we could hardly sit up in the pew.

As we waited for the service to begin, I saw that Jane was even more bushed than I was. She sat with her eyes closed as if in deep meditation, swaying occasionally in the pew.

Then Lou Hess, the dynamic young minister, stood up to announce the opening hymn: "Power! Power! Pentecostal Power! Come on, folks, give it everything you've got!"

Jane did. She even managed to get one eye open just wide enough to meet mine. Suddenly we were convulsed.

The same things always seemed to strike us funny. When we weren't laughing, we could be very serious—mostly about the Lord.

I was not long in deciding that Jane had deeper spiritual insight than any girl I had ever known; but she didn't really understand me. She revealed that on our fifth date when we were walking down Park Avenue, and she remarked, "Harald, I've been trying to figure out what kind of a husband you would make."

"Tell me, I'd like to know—a good one, I'm sure."

"You're the kind of man who would get totally engrossed in what he was doing, then suddenly wake up at eight o'clock in the evening to the fact that he had a little wife at home waiting dinner for him."

"Well, Jane, if you haven't yet learned to think of me as a perfect husband, at least you're thinking of me as a husband. I like that ... and speaking of marriage—"

"Harald, look!" She tugged at my arm and pointed. Across the street, a huge dog was rushing headlong down the sidewalk, and behind him, holding onto his leash with both hands, was a plump middle-aged dowager. Her hat was askew, and her face was a violent purple as she hollered, "Stop, Maxie, stop!" Both of us doubled up with laughter on the spot.

A moment later we were serious again, but not on the subject of marriage. Somehow, the conversation had gotten sidetracked to Jane's work, and she was telling me about a very ticklish problem she faced. I wondered if she had deftly switched, and at the same time I marveled at the frank, open way she could talk about her feelings and attitudes. She was so devoid of "front," it was a joy to be with her.

I dated her as often as I could find her free, about one-tenth as much as I would have liked to. It was because she was so special to me that I rushed over to Biblical Seminary where she lived as soon as I left the World Council office.

Her voice sounded surprised when I called her from the seminary lobby. But with a lilt of laughter, she said, "I'll be right down."

A moment later, she appeared. As we walked toward the lounge, I hoped our favorite sofa would be empty. It was. Better yet, there was no one in sight.

"Well, Harald, it's good to see you."

"Jane, the most wonderful thing has happened!"

"You've met the right girl!"

"Nothing like that. I have received the *Baptism!*"

"The what?"

"The Baptism in the Holy Spirit. I've got to tell you about it!" I told her the whole story of how God had called me to reach world leaders and that very night had started me on a quest for the Baptism, which He had finally given me at Green Lane.

When I was through, she looked full into my face and took a long, deep breath. "Well ... so you're going to reach world leaders, and now God has given you the power to do it."

"Yes, isn't it wonderful?"

"Harald, *please* don't go around telling this to everyone. I really believe that you've had a tremendous experience with the Holy Spirit. But this 'world leaders' business sounds—well, I don't know how to say it—I guess it sounds anything but humble."

"But God called me, I'm sure of that. I asked Him to make Himself *real,* to lead me like a little child, and to open the doors. He's done the first two, and He's doing the third!"

"But *is* He? You sound like you're trying to open them yourself."

"Jane, the door to reaching leaders opens when I go to work with Abram Vereide."

"Does it, Harald? Does God always work: one, two, three?"

"In this case He will."

"Time will tell, I suppose. But if God doesn't open the door, Harold, I'm afraid you're not going to see it until you run smack against it."

She held out her hand. "It was nice of you to drop by. I wish ... well, I wish you all the best."

Despite her questions, I left in high spirits. Now that I had received the Baptism in the Holy Spirit, I had no doubts that God would open up every door that needed opening.

When Dr. Knapp returned from Europe, he called me into his office. His face showed puzzled but friendly concern.

"What's this I'm hearing about you, Harald? You went off to a Pentecostal camp. And now you think you can't work here anymore. What's happened to you?" I told him the whole story and ended by saying, "And now God has called me to go back to these very leaders that we got as sponsors for the World Council and lead them to Jesus."

"I admire your zeal." He said it with a warm smile that made me realize again what a nice man he really was. "But let's not be precipitous about this. We have some exciting plans for you: setting up these promotional programs in each of the 57 countries in which we have member councils. It's an opportunity I wouldn't throw overboard too quickly if I were you. You could make it your life's career, you know.

"Harald, I'm going to do something for you I've never done before. I'm putting you on a consultant basis, earning full salary for three months. It will express our appreciation for what you have accomplished here, and it will give you time to think."

Still smiling, he reached across the desk and shook my hand. I found myself wondering, as I had a hundred times before, how a man with such a liberal theology could be such a wonderful man to work under, one of the finest men I'd ever met. I was so green when he had taken me on, and he had trained me with such patience. I felt a twinge of sadness at leaving him. I left the office, grateful for all I had learned there, but knowing that I would never be back as a working staff member. God's plans for me to take over the mantle of Abram Vereide seemed altogether too clear.

Vereide had a working pattern he had perfected through long use: "One way to lead leaders to the Living Water is to draw them to the water hole with a salt lick." He used the salt lick of other world leaders. He would draw them by inviting some big name to speak at the Harvard Club, or some such prestigious place, on a Christian topic. Then he would get a top-drawer man to issue invitations to other top-drawer men in commerce and industry to come and hear him.

My first assignment was to work with Vereide on a luncheon at the Wall Street Club, with Charles Wilson, president of General Electric, as the speaker.

That day at 11:55, the club's large dining room was almost empty. Precisely at the stroke of 12, it looked as if all the greats of American big business were pouring through the door. I counted 153 and took a seat at the back of the room, feeling really excited about the whole thing. We weren't asking for money; we weren't exploiting these men; we would be telling them about Jesus! I looked down the long table and scanned the faces ... Chester Bernard, president of Bell Telephone ... Harvey Bullis, chairman of the board of Standard Oil of New Jersey ... Howard Porter, president of North American Portland Cement ... Henry Jackson, president of General Foods ... There they were, the same men I had enlisted for the World Council. Now they would hear the gospel, and some of them would find Jesus, just as I had told Dr. Knapp they would.

Charles Wilson rose to his feet. For the first 15 minutes he entertained. Halfway through, when he made a reference to the Bible, I sat up in expectation, waiting for him to bring forth the Word of the Lord, waiting for the power to come through. Then, all of a sudden, his speech ended. His whole talk had been given without ever mentioning the need all of us have for Jesus Christ in our lives and businesses. Everyone applauded, the luncheon ended, and the guests filed out.

My spirit had never felt so grieved. Why had we gone to all the work of gathering them together? As far as I could see, not one person had been reached for Jesus. Vereide tried to reassure me by saying, "After all, this is only a curtain-raiser." But to me, it was cold comfort.

My hope had rekindled by the following week as I sat in the dining room of the Prince George Hotel in New York, having breakfast with Vereide and Ernest Williams, a member of the directing staff of the British Admiralty, and our latest "drawingcard," Norway's great war hero, Christian Oftedahl, whose father had been Norway's prime minister. He himself was a Nobel Peace Committeeman who had led the Norwegian underground during the war and had found Jesus in a Nazi prison.

What a saintly face he had! He was to be our next speaker, and I felt sure that he would not let us down. But as the morning went on, the conversation was about all the things I'd had my fill of at the World Council: approaches, underwriting and sponsorship. It seemed to me that we were trying to work with our own power, without tapping the power of God. It was distressing because I believed in what the power of God could do. Finally I found myself saying, "Gentlemen, God says it's 'not by might, nor by power, but by My Spirit.' If we will wait on God for an enduement of His power and His leadership in this, we won't have to rely so heavily on human effort!"

In an eminently civil rebuff, Ernest Williams said, "Yes, yes, that's right ... Now what were you saying, Dr. Oftedahl?"

As soon as I could get out of there, I excused myself and left. My spirits were dragging around my feet. For a few dark moments I wondered about the Holy Spirit and even my whole experience with the Baptism, tongues and the power of God.

As I crossed the lobby to the chair where I had left my hat, I found in its place a lovely dark-complexioned woman. I felt a sudden urge to talk to her. It turned out that she was an Egyptian heiress who had come to this country to settle an estate in a New York court.

As we talked, my doubts fell away, and I thought, *Wouldn't it bewonderful if this Mohammedan society belle could return to Egypt as a glowing witness for Jesus!* But how could I bring up the subject? It was like rowing around a high-cliffed island; she appeared so sophisticated and worldly that there was just no place to land. *Lord,* I silently prayed, *if You want to reach her, You are going to have to do it, because I'm stumped.* Suddenly, to my astonishment, I heard myself saying, "Have you ever heard this language before?" and I began to worship God in tongues.

Amazement filled her face. She blurted, "Where in the world did you learn archaic Arabic?"

"Before I tell you," I replied, "I want you to write down what I say."

I handed her a pad and pencil, and she wrote down 40 or 50 words as I spoke them. Then she said, "Now you *must* tell me; foreigners study Arabic for years, and we laugh at their accent. But you have no trace of one; you sound like a Bedouin saying his prayers. Were you born in Egypt?"

I took her into the sixteenth chapter of Mark: "These signs shall follow them that believe ... in my name ... they shall speak with new tongues." I said to her, "Do you believe this?"

"Indeed I do. I may be an Egyptian, but I'm not a Muslim. I'm a Catholic of the ancient Uniate Rite. My mother loved Jesus. She was always talking about Him, though much to my embarrassment, I'm afraid. She died two years ago, and I've come to see how desperately I need what she had. So far, I've only found it on the outside. Inside—" she pointed to her heart—"I'm cold and dead. Can you tell me how to make it happen here?"

I shared Jesus with her, and then with her sister, who joined us a moment later.

My own heart leaped within me. It was the power of the Holy Spirit that had brought me together with this well-traveled young lady so that I could win her for Jesus; it was the power that

I had just tried to tell them about at breakfast. I wished Vereide, Williams and Oftedahl could have seen this demonstration of what we had just been talking about.

Just then, I felt a hand on my shoulder. "By the way, Harald—"

I turned around, and there were all three men!

She began to tell them about what had happened, finishing by saying that she and her sister intended to gather their friends around the Bible at every opportunity on their Mediterranean travels.

Vereide, Williams and Oftedahl stood and listened, speechless. I did, too, for I realized that God had just given me a glimpse of what it could be like one day.[2]

---

[2] Years later, when I was challenged on whether tongues could be a recognizable language, Abraham Vereide was kind enough to testify to this event. In a letter dated March 22, 1965, he wrote: "Dear Harald, I am happy to say that I was one of the three men who came on the scene while you were witnessing to an Egyptian. She was expressing amazement at hearing

The events of the day had additional meaning for me. Up to that time, I hadn't dared tell my father of my encounter with the Holy Spirit. Now, with a witness like Abram Vereide, I finally could. I poured out my whole experience onto paper and walked to the mailbox with it that night.

In three days I had a letter back, airmail, special delivery:

> My Dear Boy—
>
> I can't tell you how grieved I am by your letter. It is obvious that you are suffering from schizophrenia and delusions of grandeur. I beg you ... see a psychoanalyst immediately.

As discouraging as my father's answer was, it didn't come close to the

---

you pray in Archaic Egyptian. Though I do not speak in tongues myself, I do recognize this incident as a demonstration of the occurrence of known languages in the glossalalia phenomenon. The two men with me were Ernest Williams, a member of the Archbishop of Canterbury's Commission on Evangelism, and Christian Qftedahl, a member of the Nobel Peace Prize Committee."

discouragement I felt later when I tried to reach leaders for Jesus. On one particular day I had made a 9A.M. appointment with Edgar Ellis, a top New York marketing executive, who had given generously to the World Council. It was my hope to witness to this man and bring him to Jesus.

Right at nine, Bible under my arm, I checked in with the receptionist and took a seat in Ellis's plush gold-and-black waiting room. At ten o'clock I checked with her again. Finally at 10:30 I was led into another office, and there I waited while a young woman took dictation over the phone. At 11:15 she hung up and asked me if I would be a little more explicit about my reasons for seeing Mr. Ellis.

"I'm a minister, and I'd like to talk to him."

"Can you give me an idea of the purpose of your visit?"

"It's personal. I'd like to speak with him myself."

"I see. If you'd like to take a seat in the waiting room, I'll notify you when he's free."

At 1:00, after many others had come and gone, I was still sitting in the plush gold chair. At 2:30 I left, without ever getting past what must have been his third assistant secretary. It was the same, day after day. I found reaching leaders for Jesus more difficult than I had ever imagined, far more difficult than enlisting them for public relations purposes.

It was obvious that other men had made it into Mr. Ellis's inner sanctum. I could have, too, if I had been a businessman. It occurred to me then, though I never did stop to check with God, that perhaps I could reach far more men for Jesus if I had a business reason for getting into their offices. Just at that time, I met Charles Freeman, a retired admiral, who, despite his 73 years, was as lean and hard-driving as he had been in the years when he had commanded the Northwest Sea Frontier. After his retirement, he had for one year been the president of William L. Hunt Corporation, a leading American firm in China. I also met Bill Kuo, a stocky Chinese engineer representing the China Import-Export Company, another China-based firm, headed by Madame Chiang Kai-shek's brother.

The three of us decided to start a company, based in the Empire State Building, to be known as Foreign Trade Corporation. My brother Norman, who had just sold a surplus war-vessel to the Indonesian government, advanced me 600 dollars to buy one-third of the stock. Bill Kuo and Admiral Freeman put up the bulk of the working capital. My titles would be Secretary-Treasurer of Foreign Trade Corporation, and Vice President of China Import-Export Company, our overseas correspondent.

Our seventieth-floor suite looked down on Fifth Avenue with a view of the East River in the distance. Admiral Freeman, with his elegant taste, furnished it himself and hung the antique white walls with a few choice paintings.

So here I was, almost before I knew it, in August 1947, an ordained Lutheran minister and one-third owner of an international business with an executive suite on the seventieth floor of the Empire State Building. Looking at my business card, no one could know that

Foreign Trade Corporation was, in fact, a precariously undercapitalized, three-man, two-room operation.

I wrote my father in great excitement:

> Dear Dad:
>
> Admiral Freeman, Bill Kuo, and I have formed a business called Foreign Trade Corporation. We are the American correspondents of one of the leading firms of China and have a suite of offices in the Empire State Building. Don't you see, Dad? God has given this to me as a base for reaching New York business leaders! Only God could have done it...

Dad replied:

> Dear Harald:
>
> When are you going to fulfill your broken vows and become a Lutheran pastor?

My reply to his letter indicated precisely where I was along the path of spiritual maturity:

> Dear Dad:
>
> The Lutheran church is built on the broken vows of a Catholic monk...

I went to see Jane to tell her about the new corporation. I was sure that it would impress her.

"So now you're in business with Madame Chiang Kai-shek's brother." She looked at me and started laughing, harder and harder. She was convulsed. "What are you going to do now, Harald," she gasped, "run China on the side?"

So Jane had laughed and Dad had doubted. I would show them both!

Almost immediately in our new corporation, I had the wonderful experience of seeing men's lives turned upside down by the experience of Jesus Christ. The first time it occurred was within the ranks of Foreign Trade Corporation itself. It was the result of an argument, one of many on the subject of truthfulness. I could be pretty sticky on the subject—"fanatical" was the word Admiral Freeman used.

There were only the three of us on the board of directors, and one day, during a board meeting, Admiral Freeman said, "Harald, be sure to record that you gave the board

24-hours' written notice of this meeting as required by law."

"How can I, when we just decided a half hour ago to have it?"

"Yes, but all three of us were here, so what's the difference? The intent of the law has been fulfilled."

"Admiral, to say something was done that wasn't done is lying!"

The Admiral, who had a very short fuse, was furious. He looked at me as if he wanted to say, "Throw that man in the brig."

I stood my ground.

Whenever the Admiral and I had an argument, which was quite often, Bill was always the peacemaker. I called him my "Admiral Handler." I didn't know it then, but the Admiral thought of him as his "Harald Handler." Bill said, "I agree with Admiral. It's all right be honest, but Harald, you too honest."

I still stood my ground.

Afterward Bill said, "Harald, you *are* too honest. That's why I don't want to become Christian. In business, you cannot succeed if you be too honest."

So Bill was just a "fellow-traveler"—not a Christian after

all. If I was sticky before, I was impossible now.

The whole thing came to a head two weeks later. Admiral Freeman had a wonderful old-world way about him that seemed to say, "We don't really need your business; we're here to serve you." It might have been effective at another point in history, but in a flourishing postwar economy, the competition was not so nonchalant. Other companies offered deals and bargains and highpressured our business contacts right out from under our noses. One by one, all of our plans turned to ashes.

The Admiral, Bill and I were sitting around his desk in the inner office trying to evaluate our mistakes when Admiral Freeman said, "Boys, unless we have a breakthrough soon, we are going to have to go out of business."

He was interrupted by the opening of the door in the outer office. We looked and there was a little old lady standing inside the door. "She's probably looking for the restroom," I muttered.

Then I looked again; there was something familiar about her ... it was

Mrs. Petricelli! We had met in the elevator a week earlier, and as we had walked out to the street together, she had told me about her son, an American major who had stayed on in Italy after the war. He had persuaded the Italian government to grant him a license to open a factory for the production of fluorescent lights. Now she was representing him in this country.

Two days later, Admiral Freeman had secured a contract from an American producer of the equipment needed in fluorescent light production, making FTC its agent, and within a week he had a firm order from Mrs. Petricelli for Italy's first factory for the production of fluorescent lights. This, the biggest order we had ever had, would save us from certain disaster. After she had signed the papers, we could hardly wait for her to get out the door so we could vent our excitement.

Ten minutes later she was back. "Oh, there is just one more little detail," she said to me. "The invoices—we want two sets, one for our records, and one for the Customs officials."

"Of course. We always give duplicates," I assured her.

"That's the point: I don't want duplicates. I want special invoices made out for Customs—at half the actual amount. The Customs officials won't look at them too carefully; we're taking care of them. We just need your cooperation."

I was aghast. The future of our company depended on this sale. But I knew I had to say, "I'm very sorry, madam, God is Senior Partner in this firm, and we couldn't do anything that would grieve Him."

"God! What's God got to do with it? I believe in God, too, young man, but God is God, and business is business!"

Suddenly this warm, motherly woman had become hard as nails. "If you don't appreciate our business, I'll take it to a firm that does. It won't be hard to find!"

"Well, madam, that's your privilege, but—" Just then, Bill emerged from the other room where he had been listening. He walked over to the irate woman, his face beaming reassurance. His hands pressed together in front of him in an almost angelic pose, he bowed deeply and rapidly to her. He could not have been more ingratiating and obsequious had she been a Mandarin. She stared at him, fascinated. Her face relaxed.

Now, with an expression of deep, warm concern, he said, "Lady, we want help you."

Stunned, I said, "Okay, Bill, I wash my hands of this thing," and walked out of the room. Feeling righteously indignant, I listened as Bill and the lady worked out the horrid details. As she went out the door, I could hear her repeating, "Now, remember, at 7:55 tomorrow morning, my taxi will be taking me past here on the way to the ship. I'll have but a moment to pick up those invoices."

"You leave to me. I take care ... I take care."

When Bill passed my desk, I refused to look up, but he stopped and said, "Harald, you *are* too honest." He had said that many times, but this time he went on, "Maybe someday I be honest, too."

Could something be happening to Bill? I felt better.

The next morning when I came into my office, he was waiting for me, his face radiant. He looked as if he had seen a vision.

"Harald, last night I become Christian."

"You did? What happened?"

"I wait till late at night to type up invoices. I could not ask secretary do it, she Christian. I all alone. Wind howling in elevator shaft. God, He speak to me."

"What did He say, Bill?"

"He say, 'Bill, you know that invoice phony.' I say, 'Yes, Lord, I know invoice phony, but I promise lady. Must keep promise ... but, Lord, this is last time I ever be dishonest. After this, I be too honest, like Harald.'"

"What did you do, Bill?"

"I type up phony invoice, all right, but at top I type in special serial number, 'UT 895.'"

"What did the UT stand for?"

He looked at me as if surprised at having to explain. "Why, 'untrue,' of course."

"Bill, that was still dishonest."

"I sorry. I promise never again."

True to his word, Bill never again did anything else in the business that was dishonest in any way. And from this extremely shaky beginning, Bill grew to become a beautiful, Spirit-filled Christian.

But I had failed God. I had thought that by protesting this fraud and washing my hands of it, I could escape the guilt of it, but I could not. By not doing everything in my power to prevent it, I was as responsible as the other two—in fact, more so, because I knew better.

If I had said, "Bill, write those invoices and I resign," he probably would have backed down, and if he had not, all I would have lost would have been my job, and God would have provided a better one. But part of me *wanted* Bill to write those invoices and "save" the company. I wanted to protest his dirty work, and at the same time enjoy the fruit of it.

God, through years of excruciatingly painful lessons, finally taught me that the moment I have to compromise to retain a position, it is an indication that He does not intend me to remain in that position.

It is humiliating to realize how long it took me to learn that lesson, but praise God, He never gives up on us! He brings us around again and again to the truth we have been trying to escape until we are finally willing to face it.

Each day it seemed as if God was bringing across my path someone whose heart He had prepared for an encounter with Himself—even though outwardly they might not seem at all ready. The day George Eversfield came to my office, he seemed anything but ready. A cocksure, aristocratic young British businessman, George had left his job as sales manager of a rather large British steel firm to move to the States. His sophistication and *savoir faire* were almost overwhelming. He sat in the office and talked about everything under the sun, and all the while I was looking for an opening to tell him about Jesus. Not being able to find one, I suddenly interjected, "George, what do you think of Jesus Christ?"

Half-laughing, he said, "Who knows? A myth perhaps?"

"Would you like to know?"

"Why, sure."

I took him into the third chapter of Revelation, the twentieth verse, and we read together, "Behold, I stand at the door and knock. If any man will hear my voice and open the door, I will come in." I said, "George, what does Jesus say He's doing here?"

"Well, He says He's standing at the door of my heart seeking admittance."

"Is He?"

"How can you know?"

"You can't know whether someone is outside your door until you open the door and see if He's there."

"That makes sense, but how do you open the door?"

"Well, as an agnostic, you can't approach Jesus as a fact. You must approach Him as a hypothesis and pray a hypothetical prayer. 'Jesus, whoever You are, whatever You are, *if* You are, come into my heart and reveal Yourself to me. And if You do, I'll serve You.'" I added, "Be sure to include that final clause, 'If You do, I'll serve You,' otherwise there would be no point to His revealing Himself to you. Would you be willing to pray that prayer, George?"

"Sure."

"Okay. Let's get down on our knees and pray it."

"Oh, I could never pray here in this office."

"When will you pray?"

"Tonight. At nine o'clock."

"Okay. We'll be praying for you."

The following week George told me the story of that night. "I was rather tired and decided to knock off early. I had just gotten into bed when the tower clock outside struck nine times. I thought, 'Oh-oh, nine o'clock. I've got an appointment.' So I got out of bed and down on my knees and prayed this prayer: 'Jesus, whoever You are, whatever You are, if You are, come into my heart and reveal Yourself to me, and if You do, I'll serve You.'

"I felt nothing, but I thought, 'Well, at least I've kept my part of the bargain.' To my own surprise, during the next three days I read practically the whole New Testament you gave me. Then a few nights later, I had just gotten into bed when suddenly great cleansing waves rolled over me. It was just as if the entire burden of my guilt was lifted. I hadn't had any sense of guilt before at all, so I never realized how heavy the load I was carrying was until it was lifted. I felt as clean and innocent as a newborn baby. And God spoke to me. 'You have just been born into the family of God. Just as a child must grow in the likeness of his parents, so you must grow in the likeness of Jesus Christ. Feed on My Word.'"

George grew by leaps and bounds, and two years later, Mrs. Aymar Johnson, a cousin of President Roosevelt, sent him back to England to speak to the International Christian Leadership group in Parliament and to work among the British elite. Later he returned to this country and began a ministry in New England. The last I had heard of him, he had founded six churches.

So, two men had come to Jesus. This was only the beginning. There would be others, I was sure of that.

# 10

On the outside, it still looked as if everything was going according to plan. We had our beautiful office situation, I was still with Vereide, and we had our groups going at the Harvard Club, the Princeton Club, and the Chamber of Commerce. Actually, however, the finances of the corporation were not going according to plan at all. I knew from reading Christian success stories that they were like real-life Horatio Alger tales, stories that usually went, "I was going bankrupt, when I handed my company over to God" or "I decided to tithe, and God has now made me a multimillionaire." I had read a lot of books on economic success through spiritual motivation, one might say, and I knew it worked for others. But it certainly wasn't working for us at Foreign Trade Corporation.

As time went on, it grew more and more apparent that Admiral Freeman was not a businessman. It's one thing to command a fleet and another thing to run a business. Neither Bill Kuo nor

I had any real business experience, and except for the fluorescentlight order, we had sold very little. It seemed that we would be right on the brink of a tremendous killing, but it would nearly always fall through.

And then, on top of everything else, there was the thing we had been most counting on: our role as correspondent for one of the leading firms of China. At the time we started the company, Generalissimo Chiang Kai-shek was pushing the Communists into the sea, and the doors for commerce between the United States and China were opening wide. Then, almost overnight, the whole thing was reversed, and it was the Generalissimo who was being washed into the sea. Our Chinese correspondent firm had been all but knocked out by the Communists, and we were deprived of what was to have been the mainstay of our business.

Because our finances were so precarious, it was agreed that we wouldn't draw any salary until the company was properly capitalized. I went along with this, even though I had no money at all of my own, because I didn't want them to consider me the weak member of the team. Although I continued to come to work each day at a splendid office, and hobnobbed with big wheels at the best New York clubs, I was, in reality, destitute.

The terrible part was that my mother sensed how bad things were and would sneak me the extra money that Uncle Harold sent her. I lived in the slums, paying five dollars a week room and board to Emma Fowler, the elderly woman who had been praying for me from the very moment I had surrendered my life to God. Since she was on relief, my corner of her apartment made that first room at the Y seem palatial. It was a tiny cubicle overlooking a garbage-strewn court, with a bed that was no more than a cot. A few boxes of books stood in the corner, covered with the dust that seemed to be everywhere. My only furniture was a desk and a three-legged chair.

As if it wasn't bad enough to live like this and have Mother guess it, I came home one night and found a terse note waiting for me from Dad.

Dear Harald,

By now you must realize that you have *missed* the boat. Why don't you stop showing off, admit your failure, and step out?

Pinned to the paper was a 20-dollar bill.

I wondered how my father, too, had guessed my need. Certainly I never admitted to anyone my situation. On the contrary, I put up a fantastic front. The Glenwood, Iowa, farm community where my folks still lived was so close-knit that even in 1948 the favorite method of communication was for the whole area to listen in on the party line. Frequently I called Dad long-distance and raved about the souls coming to Christ, the great expectations I had for our business, and the famous people I knew, including, of course, the millionaires. I knew that all of Glenwood was listening and, at the same time, being forced to agree that their boy Harald had made good in the big city. And now Dad saw through my façade and wanted me to know that he did. That 20-dollar bill became a symbol of his disapproval. I felt my whole body tense as I held it between my fingers, but as much as I wanted to, I couldn't mail it back, because Miss Fowler and I were out of food, and I owed 15 dollars of it to her.

With incredible irony, the next day at the office Admiral Freeman said, "Congratulations, Harald. You're the new president of Foreign Trade Corporation."

"Great!" Then I found out why. In our postwar economy, with its tremendous shortages, we were being sued for failure to deliver the 5,000 kegs of nails we had promised to provide but could not due to the bankruptcy of our supplier. The Admiral wanted to protect his personal assets by cutting his legal ties with the firm.

In addition to being sued, there were many other problems, until I didn't know which way to turn. Instead of going to bed one night, I paced back and forth in my little room, wondering if it had been folly to leave the World Council.

When I woke up the following morning, I was so sick and feverish I couldn't even get out of bed and go to work. I lay in the cold room, staring at the curtain over the doorway, wishing for the luxury of a door so that Miss Fowler would not see how sick I was. By afternoon I forced myself to sit up and make phone contacts, trying my best to drum up some business.

I had just begun my tenth call—"Sir, I represent Foreign Trade Corporation, and I'd like to make an appointment to see you—" when Miss Fowler pushed aside the curtain and showed one of my closest friends from seminary into my room. He had been to our beautiful office in the Empire State Building to look me up, and they had given him my address.

He was obviously as horrified at finding me in such circumstances as I was at being found. I tried desperately to think of an explanation that would not make me an object of pity, but could not.

Bob didn't say anything. He just stood there, his eyes taking in the surroundings. There was stunned amazement on his face.

"Pull up a chair, but be careful—" I tried to make a joke of it "—it only has three legs."

"No, no, thank you. Um, I just thought I'd stop by and say hello." He kept looking at me as if he couldn't believe the abject poverty that I was living in.

"Bob, it's good to see you. I'll tell you what. As soon as I'm up and around, I want you to be my guest for lunch at the Harvard Club."

"Fine, Harald." He backed out of the room, and I heard his footsteps through the apartment and hurrying down the hall.

I listened until his steps faded, and then I rolled over to face the wall and groaned. Realizing I was still holding the phone in my hand, I hung it up, too sick to even try to make another contact.

As I closed my eyes, I could see two demonic eyes come together into one eye, and from then on I refused to sleep, because whenever I closed my eyes, they were there. My fever, accompanied by dysentery, grew worse and worse, until one of my friends, Cyril Mouland, came over and said, "Harald, you have a raging fever. You've got to go to the hospital."

"I don't have any money, and I'm not going to embarrass my family."

"But you could die here."

"I really don't care if I do. If God wants to heal me, He'll heal me. If He doesn't want to heal me, okay. I don't care." I was almost glad to put God on the spot, because I felt He had let me down.

Cyril turned around and walked out. I remember Miss Fowler coming in with water and begging me to drink it, but I was too sick to swallow. Then Cyril came back with an ambulance attendant. "Come on. You're going to the hospital."

I moaned. "I'm not going. I don't have the money, and I'm not going into debt."

"Mr. Birch is taking care of everything."

Frank R. Birch was the multimillionaire president of a major advertising agency. He had been reading the Gospel of John, to study the advertising psychology of Jesus, when he had fallen on his knees and accepted Him as his Savior. I had introduced Cyril to him, and he had underwritten the founding of a mission, with Cyril as director and myself as secretary-treasurer. Christian Soldiers Mission, as Mr. Birch had called it, was his pride and joy. Often he would bring in his friends, among them J.C. Penney who loved to put his arms around a derelict and bring him to the altar. While Frank grew in the Lord, his wife, Emily, acted as though he was going through a phase. And she would indulge him.

She and I hit it off very well together until one night she told me, "I'll make heaven because of all the good I've done." With singular lack of tact, I asked her, "Emily, do you know what Saint Peter is going to say to you when you ask him to let you in?"

"Tell me."

"Mrs. Birch, you are just about the nicest lady we've ever turned away from these gates."

"Why?"

"Because you have just told me that you are relying on all your good works rather than the Blood of Christ for your salvation."

From then on, she resented me. Nevertheless, Frank Birch remained my friend, and since I had neither asked him nor hinted for the money, I felt free to accept his offer to pay, believing that it was the provision of the Lord.

At the hospital, I heard Cyril say, "Spare no expense. A millionaire is behind him."

At the end of the week, the bill was fantastic, and I said, "Send it to Mr. Mouland. He'll take it to Mr. Birch." The next day the hospital secretary came to my bedside and somewhat abashedly informed me, "Mr. Birch refuses to pay your bill."

Totally crushed, I buried my face in my pillow and kept it there, as I was moved out of my beautiful room to a charity ward. When Cyril came to visit, he told me what had happened. Emily Birch had heard her husband making arrangements for my bill, and she was furious. "The idea! What a freeloader! If you pay it, Frank, I'll never speak to you again."

"He's worked very hard for Christian Soldiers, and he really has no money."

"Well, his family does."

So when Mr. Birch refused to pay the bill, Cyril got on the phone to my dad. And to the listening ears of all Glenwood, he said, "Harald is absolutely penniless. He is in critical condition in the hospital and doesn't have a cent to pay for his room."

Just like that, all the front was stripped away. I could have cried in bitter humiliation. Uncle Harold flew up from Washington to see me and said that Admiral Freeman had told him my Pentecostalism and my all-night prayer meetings were responsible for my condition. My mother flew in and brought with her, to my utter and final degradation, a generous collection of money from the people of Glenwood.

During the 10 days I spent on the critical list, my condition had grown steadily worse. The doctor said, "We can't seem to stop your fever. Everything has failed. We've even pumped you full of a new wonder drug, which is supposed to cure everything, but it hasn't helped you."

"Good. That means that we'll just have to let God do it. If He wants to heal me, that's fine. If He doesn't, that's fine too." From then on, I refused all medicine.

While I was lying there, too sick to care, the door opened and in came Jane. She was like an angel. She reached for my hand. There was such balm in her touch. In contrast to Admiral Freeman's and Uncle Harold's stern-faced condemnation, there was only compassion and loving concern in her voice and face. "Harald, I'm sorry you're sick." And I knew she really was. She prayed then, sweetly and softly. I closed my eyes, and when I opened them, she was gone.

The very next day, for the first time, I felt well enough to sit up by myself. From then on, I grew steadily stronger. The doctor said, "We believe you were being poisoned by the new drug, and by refusing medicine, you've saved your own life." Whether it was that or Jane's prayer, in three days I was allowed to leave the hospital and return to Glenwood with Mother for three months of rest.

It was so good to be out of New York and away from Foreign Trade Corporation, and so good to look out of the window of my room and see trees and rolling hills instead of garbage cans, that I hardly minded the humiliation of being back under my parents' roof. Day by day, with Mother's good Norwegian cooking, I grew stronger and stronger.

As I gained in strength, I could think of nothing but Jane, beautiful Jane, Jane the angel at my bedside. My love and desire for her was now as raging as the fever had been. Finally I could wait no longer. I picked up a pen and proposed to her by mail. Day after day, I waited for her reply. I awoke one particularly cold and snowy morning, and I *knew* I would hear from her that day. When the mailman's car pulled away, I skipped, almost running down the long driveway, oblivious to the biting cold. When I opened the mailbox, her letter lay there like a golden prize. For an instant I stood there, holding it in my hand, savoring the moment. Then I ripped it open, holding my breath while I read.

Dear Harald,

Your letter arrived this morning. What a great tribute you have paid me. I, too, cherish the memory of our good times together. And, Harald, I love you, but only like a brother...

"Only like a brother..." My heart seemed to stop. My love for her was as living and pulsating as love could be. It was anything but brotherly. I dragged back to the house, numb with cold and disappointment. I picked up my Bible for some word of comfort, some explanation as to what the meaning of this was. It fell open to a verse in Hebrews: "Cast not away, therefore, your confidence, which hath great recompense of reward. For ye have need of patience that, after ye have done the will of God, ye might receive the promise."

I sighed, relieved and reassured. God was only testing my patience. I didn't mind waiting for Jane, as long as God was saving her for me.

From that moment on, I had one desire—to get well enough to return to New York so that I could tell her in person that we really were meant for each other, and show her the proof. The moment I arrived back, I went straight over to Biblical Seminary to find her. She was surprised. "Why, Harald—"

In a rush, I told her what God had promised me. She shook her head. "I know this is going to hurt, Harald, but I must tell you. I'm engaged. His name is Peter." Seeing what must have been a stricken expression, she tried to console me. "Harald, he reminds me so much of you."

It was little comfort. I managed some meaningless conversation for a few minutes and then withdrew. But before I had gone half a block, I was filled with a rush of happiness. God had promised Jane to me, and now He was just testing my faith. What was I worried about? He would see that Jane would someday be mine.

My spirits were still buoyant when I arrived at the office of Foreign Trade Corporation. Bill Kuo met me in the outer office. He bowed in a warm welcoming manner and then clapped me on the back. "Harald, we've got good news for you. I'll let Admiral Freeman tell you." He led me into where the Admiral was looking over a display stand of a new invention. It was something that I had just been reading about in *Reader's Digest,* a magnetic tape recorder. "It's our new line," the Admiral said. "It's going over very well. In fact, you might say it's the salvation of Foreign Trade Corporation."

"And the lawsuit?" I asked.

"They dropped that. As our attorney pointed out to them, you can't get blood out of a turnip."

"In that case, I'll give you back your old job as president."

"No, we're leaving you there, and what is more, you're actually going to receive a salary," he chuckled. "I've gotten a promotion, too; I'm the new chairman of the board."

It was great to be back and have hope of a future. I'd brought with me the determination to succeed as no one else had ever succeeded. I sat down at my old desk, itching to get back to work and vindicate myself before Glenwood, as well as Mom and Dad.

What's more, I was going to prove to Jane that God's hand was mightily upon me.

It wasn't long before I discovered that wealthy foreign visitors were the people most captivated by these magical boxes called tape recorders. They would buy them on sight and in quantity. I decided that in order to sell the device, I had to expose it to as many people from abroad as possible. A brilliant idea came to me. What better way to meet these newcomers than the one place almost all visitors came to: the observation deck of the Empire State Building. I took the tape recorder up there and interviewed at random a man from Australia.

"How do you like New York City?"

"Good show up here, man."

"How long will you be here?"

"Four days."

"Why did you come?"

"Well, you see, there's this possibility..."

When he was through with his story, I asked, "How would you like to hear your voice?"

"Eh?"

I rewound the tape and played it back. He listened, his face glowing.

"Say, that's jolly interesting," he said. "Where could I get such a device? I could use two dozen of them; in fact,

I'd like to be the distributor for Australia."

"Just stop off at the Foreign Trade Corporation on the seventieth floor. I'm sure you'll find them most cooperative."

It was such a successful idea that I was off and running with it, forgetting my main purpose for being in business.

I phoned WNYC, New York City's official radio station: "I've been interviewing visitors from abroad on top of the Empire State Building; would you like to have a tape of the most interesting interview? We could call it 'Visitor of the Week.'"

The program director was hesitant. "Well, give us a sample."

I knew that in order to sell them on the idea, this interview had to be really something.

At this time in 1948 the fighting between Israel and the Arabs had broken into open warfare, and Sweden's Count Folke Bernadotte, the U.N. mediator and a devout Christian, was in New York to report to an emergency session of the General Assembly. Why not interview him? He was the man of the hour, and the peace of the Middle

East, perhaps of the world, hinged on his efforts.

But how to reach him? I could never do it as the representative of a radio program that did not as yet exist. I thought of the "Lutheran Hour," carried every Sunday on a thousand stations around the world. I called the director, Dr. Walter Maier, and said, "Count Folke Bernadotte is, as you know, a devout Christian. Would you like to have him come on your broadcast and personally appeal to the Christians of the world to pray for his mission?" He would indeed.

Now that I was able to offer the Count a thousand-station voice to the world, I got through to him immediately.

"I am very sorry," he said. "I give interviews to no one. Every minute that I am away from Palestine, lives are being lost."

On a hunch, I called his wife, and we chatted for a while. I told her how disappointed I was in not being able to interview her husband, and in return she shared a disappointment of her own: "You know, there was an interview with me done by the New York

*DailyNews,* but when I went down to the lobby to get a copy, they were sold out."

I sympathized, hung up the phone, and dialed the *Daily News.* Putting on my most authoritative voice, I said, "Send 50 copies of today's paper to the Countess Folke Bernadotte and mark them 'from Harald Bredesen.'"

When she called me to express her thanks, she also mentioned that she had intervened with the Count on my behalf; he would give me an interview at the airport just before he caught his plane. This had to be God opening the doors. I fell on my knees and thanked Him. At last, it seemed that my dream of being in business to bring leaders to Jesus was on the verge of being realized. What's more, it was real success, heady stuff for someone who longed for it like I did.

Then, deciding to parlay it into something even more successful, I called Lowell Thomas, the most famous newscaster of the day. "Count Folke Bernadotte has agreed to give me an interview. Would you like to share it?"

Lowell Thomas was more than impressed. "That's great. Bring him out here to Pawling, and we'll interview him in my studio. Governor Dewey's right next door, and we'll ring him in on it." Dewey was at the time running for president.

But since the interview had to be at the airport, and Lowell Thomas only interviewed at his home, I called CBS with my news. I heard them say, "Hey, fellows, this guy's got Count Folke Bernadotte!" They sent one of their best men, Larry LeSourd, with me to the airport, and he interviewed for CBS. I interviewed for the "Lutheran Hour" and used it as the sample for my "Visitor of the Week."

Then Lowell Thomas called me.

"Got any more ideas?"

"Well—" I paused and thought rapidly "—General Lucius Clay is coming to Washington, D.C., for an emergency consultation with the president. What about him?" (It was the height of the crisis over the Berlin Blockade, the first major confrontation between Russia and the West. War seemed imminent.)

"That would be great. Draw me up a sample slate of questions."

I did, including one question on a religious topic. Then, with Abram Vereide's help, I was able to get General Clay to agree to an interview. There was one hitch: It would have to be in Berlin.

Lowell Thomas was impressed with both the questions and with the fact that the General had agreed to let me interview him.

"Can you perform a miracle," he said, "and leave within 24 hours for Berlin?"

But a far greater plan than that of merely interviewing one dignitary in Europe was hatching in my mind. Using the pull of my Uncle Harold, who, as chairman of the Ways and Means Committee, was now one of the most powerful men in Congress, I saw myself interviewing Churchill, Stalin, Truman, de Gaulle, and Prime Minister De Gasperi of Italy, as well as other top lead-ers, on the burning issues of the day. I planned to edit their replies together, cut my voice out, and dub Lowell Thomas in, as if he himself was asking them the questions. It would be the world's first electronic summit conference. What had originally begun as a scheme to sell tape recorders would now shake the world!

Lowell Thomas was excited, and gave me a 500-dollar retainer.

As the plan grew, so did my pride. At this juncture, I bumped into another old seminary friend. We had been classmates, prayer partners, and very close friends.

"Why, Harald, what are you doing now?"

"Oh, I'm preparing for a world tour, interviewing heads of state for the Lowell Thomas broadcast."

"Isn't that wonderful! How did that come about?"

"It's the kind of thing that happens to you when you receive the Baptism in the Holy Spirit. God opens doors that no one could *possibly* open!"

"Is that right?"

"Oh, yes! It's a chance to change the world."

"Harald, I always knew you would be the biggest success in our class."

I didn't tell him, but at that moment I could see myself standing in the Kremlin, Stalin listening white-faced and trembling as I spoke the prophecy God had given me for him: "I have heard the cry of the captive..." It was Moses and Pharaoh all over again.

I went to see Jane and tell her about my plans. Now I knew that she would recognize that God's hand was mightily upon me. What I was doing was an overwhelming demonstration of it. I was sure that she would want to be by my side when I reaped the benefits of my success. I watched her expression as I unfolded the absolutely fantastic thing God was doing. But she didn't react at all the way I expected. Instead of wondering admiration, I saw something that looked suspiciously like compassion.

"If this *is* God, that's wonderful. But if it's promotional skill, then God help you. The ground is going to come up mighty fast."

"Jane, I think this fiancé of yours—what's his name?—Peter, has made you pessimistic." Then I added,

"By the way, how is everything with you two?"

"We're getting married next month."

"Congratulations."

On the way back to the office, I shook my head. Poor Peter. He didn't have long for this world. They'd marry, and then he would go and be with the Lord. After a suitable period of mourning, Jane's eyes would be opened. She would see how fantastically God was using me and come rushing into my arms.

The next day I had a conversation with Lowell Thomas's secretary: "What is this spell you have woven over Lowell?" she asked. "I've never seen him go so overboard with a man of such short acquaintance."

"It's not me, it's the Lord. I know Lowell thinks he is sending me on this world tour, but it isn't him at all. God has called me to reach world leaders, and this is the way He has shown me to do it."

"You mean that *this* is your motive for making the world tour?"

"Certainly."

"Does Lowell know this?"

"Well ... why, no. Do you think I should tell him?"

"I think you'd better."

That night, over dinner, I made Lowell aware of my purpose. My heart was in my throat, waiting for his response.

"Wonderful. Wonderful. You'll do a better job for me if your motives aren't selfish."

At home that night I lay awake for hours, too exhilarated to sleep, reading and re-reading Lowell Thomas's letter to the State Department:

This will introduce Harald Bredesen, who will tour the world to interview, for my broadcast, heads of state and anyone, anywhere, whom he considers newsworthy.

What a platform for witness God had built for me! From it, I would be able to reach any leader in the world. I thought, *Since I'm doing all this for the glory of God, when the time comes, I will lay all this acclaim at His feet.* In my mind, I could hear the people of Glenwood finally admitting, "Isn't it marvelous! He's reached the pinnacle of success, and see how humbly he lays it all at the feet of Jesus!"

Within the week, Lowell Thomas called. "Harald, you'd better come up here; I have bad news." When I arrived, he was quite upset.

"It seems that the heads of state will not agree to be interviewed on a broadcast sponsored by Ivory Soap. It's beneath their dignity, they say, to be used in a commercial setting." I took a deep breath and tried to comprehend it all while he continued. "But here is an alternative. You can do the same thing on a public service basis. I'm going to give you a letter of introduction to America's foremost historian, Dr. Henry Steele Commager, head of the History Department at Columbia University. I'm sure Columbia will back you."

So I set off to see Dr. Commager. On the subway, I praised God for His timing. This whole thing was beginning to have a nice ring to it: *Tonight we bring you Harold Bredesen under the auspices of ColumbiaUniversity, interviewing, for the entire Free World,*

*Sir Winston Churchill!* Yes, it had a very nice ring.

Dr. Commager was enthusiastic. "This is a wonderful idea! Of course if Columbia is going to get behind it, it would be better if they think that the idea originated right here on the campus. Lowell Thomas tells me that your motives are completely un-selfish. Is that right?"

"Right!"

"The important thing to you is that the mission be accomplished." "Right."

"I take it, then, that you don't care who gets the credit, or who does the actual interviewing?"

My heart sank, and I felt my whole body go limp. All of a sudden, I realized I did care. I cared terribly. I wanted to do the interviewing, and I wanted the credit! I smiled and lamely agreed, trying my best to hide how much I hurt at the realization that Columbia would now take over the project.

I wished him the best of luck, crawled home, and stumbled onto my bed, where I groaned for hours. As I lay there, it finally came to me with devastating clearness that God wasn't interested in my project. He hadn't opened the last door, because ever since I had received the Baptism, I had been running far ahead of Him. The room grew dark as I cried, "But, God, why? I thought You called me, and I have been trying to do what I thought You wanted."

Then I heard it, the same low gentle voice that I had heard that night on the bus, only this time the words didn't command—they convicted.

"What is your motive? Your real motive? Isn't it to vindicate yourself?"

I waited a long time to answer. Finally I said, "Yes, Lord. I wanted to prove to the fellows at the seminary, the professors, my friends at the World Council, all of Glenwood, and especially my parents and Jane that I'm a spectacular success in Your service." After another long while I said, "Lord, I'm not spectacular. I'm a nobody. I tried to be somebody great, but I'm not." It hurt so much to admit aloud to myself and to God that I was a failure that I began to blubber. After a longer wait I said, "I am a nobody. But,

Lord, I'm content, no matter what anybody thinks, to be a nobody."

As I spoke, the first light of dawn came through the window, and with it, more peace than I had known in a long while.

# 11

"Harald, have you ever heard of a man named Ralph Montanus?" Violet Vogel, our secretary at Foreign Trade Corporation, had asked me this just before the time I was off and running with Lowell Thomas.

"No, I don't think so. Why?"

"He's blind. His only money is the pittance he gets from the state. And he's struggling to publish a Braille gospel quarterly and send it to blind subscribers around the world. I've been doing voluntary secretarial work for him, and I think you could help him."

"I doubt it."

"Sure you could. With your promotional background, you could help him in raising funds."

"No, thank you, Violet. I'm already mixed up in so many things I can't get involved in any more. Certainly not in money raising; I've had enough of that for a lifetime."

"Won't you come with me tonight and at least meet him? Please? Pretty please?" She fluttered her eyelids and gave me her most fetching smile.

"Not tonight—"

"How about a week from next Thursday?" I agreed, hoping that if I put it off long enough she'd forget about it. An unusual coincidence occurred that week. Joe Belgum was in Brooklyn, New York, with the Lutheran Welfare Services. One day we were having lunch when one of his fellow staff members plopped down at our table. "Say, I've got the oddest case on my hands, a blind man who is suffering from delusions of grandeur. He thinks he is going to start a worldwide ministry for the blind. He's just an ordinary kid with nothing going for him and lots of strikes against him."

Joe asked, "What's his name?"

"Ralph Montanus."

"Ralph Montanus!" I blurted. "That's the guy my secretary's been after me to help."

Joe's caseworker friend continued, "Joe, when you get back to the office, talk to this character and see what you can do with him." Then, in a winking aside to me, "Joe has a real knack with oddball characters. Maybe it's because he's such a ... such a—"

Joe, who always enjoyed a joke at his own expense, laughed. "Go ahead and finish it: '—such an oddball character himself.'"

When lunch was over, we walked back to the Lutheran Welfare office together, and I waited in Joe's office while he went in and talked to Ralph Montanus. When he returned, his face was glowing. "That man doesn't have delusions of grandeur. He *has* grandeur. Harald, why don't you see what you can do about giving him a little help?"

"I'll tell you why," I replied, savoring each word. "Because at lunch this noon a very wise friend of mine named Joe Belgum said, 'Harald, you're spreading yourself too thin.'"

He grinned. "I did, didn't I? Still..."

Even with Joe's encouragement, I would have forgotten all about Ralph, if Violet hadn't remembered our week-from-Thursday date. Reluctantly, I went with her to see him. We found him in his office, a second-floor burned-out Chinese restaurant that nobody had bothered to repair. It was as junky and drab as a Salvation Army thrift shop.

Ralph himself was a young man of about 26 with brown eyes, ash-blond hair, and average height and build. But I wondered as I looked at his face and felt his charisma how the caseworker could have described him as ordinary. His strong features and warm, compelling manner were anything but ordinary. Nor was that artesian well of exuberant confidence in God that seemed to spring up from the depths of his being. I had not been with him for five minutes before I realized that this was one of the most extraordinary young men I had ever met. I found myself agreeing with Joe: "This man *has* grandeur."

When his wife came in from the other room, he introduced her. "I would like to have you meet Bea, my right-hand man. Actually, she's my right hand." Bea was pretty and auburn haired with a warm, quiet dignity and a knack, I discerned, of making people feel at home. I liked her immediately.

As Ralph talked about his work and his vision of bringing the gospel to the blind all over the world, I began to sense the presence of God in the room. My heart began to burn within me, just as it had in Warren Morno's car. But this time, instead of filling my heart with joy, it filled me with apprehension as it came to me, *What if God has asked me to come here and cast my lot with Ralph?* I looked around the dreary setting and contrasted it with our offices in the Empire State Building. I had worked hard for that office, investing every penny I could come across and three years of my life. Now at long last, it was beginning to pay off. God certainly couldn't be asking ... Then it came to me—He wouldn't ask me to come here. His call on my life is to reach leaders. I sighed with relief. During the rest of the evening, I tried to be as encouraging as I could to Ralph without committing myself.

Shortly after that, I began running with Lowell Thomas, preparing for a world tour, and far too busy to think of a blind kid struggling to publish a Braille paper in a burned-out restaurant.

It wasn't until my last house of cards collapsed and I was finally willing to be a nobody for God that I thought of Ralph again. I went to him and promised to help him raise 300 dollars each month, the cost of putting out the *Gospel Messenger,* as he called his Braille quarterly.

As I worked with Ralph and Bea, their apartment became very special to me. It was the first floor of a slummy duplex, and Bea's big problem was the invasion of cockroaches that came down from the apartment above them. She was not only her husband's "right hand," she was a very hardworking, fastidious mother and homemaker. She used every conceivable spray and powder, but to no avail. It was like trying to sweep back the sea with a broom. Despite these unwanted guests, the prayer meetings in their kitchen were filled with the glory and splendor of God. I had never, even at Green Lane camp meeting, seen or felt anything like it. For me, that roach-infested kitchen became the most beautiful and exciting place on Earth.

Meanwhile, I continued working with Abram Vereide, who frequently came up from Washington to address the breakfast and luncheon groups he had helped us start. Though in speaking to groups he could be too low-key for my instincts, I marveled at the way he seemed to know the exact moment when a man was ready for a personal, private encounter with Jesus Christ. I was appreciating more and more the privilege of being his understudy.

One morning while leading the Bible discussion at our Harvard Club breakfast meeting, I became aware of the smiling brown eyes and lean scholarly face of a tall, bespectacled young man of about 23 who afterward introduced himself to me as Steve Hart. Seeing his interest, I invited him to walk back with me to the Empire State Building. "I was just going there anyway," he said. "My father's suite is on the seventy-third floor."

Walking down Fifth Avenue, I learned more about Steve. He was a Princetonian and had just graduated from Cornell Law School. What I learned later was that he had been among the top four in his class, that his father was president of the National Economic Council, and that he himself was heir to a large fortune. Steve's blueblood background hadn't included old slum houses, I reasoned. *Besides,* I thought, *he is a new Christian and probably not readyfor the roach test.* But on the off chance that maybe, for once, there wouldn't be any crawling insects, I agreed to take him. While we were singing, I noticed several of the long brown bugs crawling in and out from beneath the woodwork by Steve's chair. I wondered what Steve would say. He never noticed; at least he didn't let on if he did. Going home, he said, "I have a small inheritance from my grandmother. I wonder if God is telling me to help the Gospel Association for the Blind."

A week later I was up in Ralph's office when Bea's brother, Ray Butler, came running into the building. "Ralph! Ralph! Look! We got 1,000 dollars in the mail." He showed us a cashier's check and a note. Judging from the donor's grammar and penmanship, he had barely gotten through the third grade. As I wondered what ignorant person would have a thousand dollars, it came to me that this was just the kind of thing that Steve Hart would do. Later when I kidded him about it, his dark eyes turned to black steel. "Did it ever occur to you that the donor gave the money anonymously because he wanted to remain anonymous?" I apologized and never mentioned it again.

Altogether there grew to be quite a number of people putting out the *Gospel Messenger.* Besides Ralph and Bea, Steve Hart, and myself, there was Bill Kuo from Foreign Trade Corporation and three other men and their wives. Counting their children, there were about 20 of us.

At these meetings, it was not uncommon for one or another of us to receive a word of prophecy from the Holy Spirit, usually a general encouragement or exhortation for all of us. It was always a thrill to hear God speak in the first person; as Paul indicates in his first letter to the Corinthians, prophecy (unlike tongues and interpretation, which are primarily a sign to the nonbeliever) is meant to help the believer.

One night while we were praying and waiting upon the Lord, we received an unusually explicit prophecy instructing us to found a New Testament church and to have all things in common as did the Early Christians. We pooled our resources—money, cars, debts, furniture, everything—and leased a triplex apartment house. Steve Hart put in 22,000 dollars and his grandmother's diamond brooch. (Later, when he came into his inheritance, he put over a million dollars into Christian work abroad.) Out of the pool of money, we assigned ourselves 15 dollars each as a weekly allowance.

Living "in community" became a time of self-discovery and, even more painful, self-uncovery. It's easy to keep your best foot forward for a couple of hours in a Christian fellowship meeting, but you can't live 24 hours a day with your best foot forward. Eventually, that other foot is bound to come out for all to see and for all to deal with. The women, I found, were amazingly unselfish, until it came to their children. Once when someone gave us two cribs—one bright and new, the other old and shabby—the women growled at each other for days because each felt her child should have the new one.

My own selfishness came out in a lot of seemingly trivial little ways, for example, in my reluctance to clean the office bathroom. The women cleaned the apartment bathrooms, but the office bathroom was not their responsibility. As a result, it grew dirtier and smellier each day, waiting for someone to take his turn cleaning.

The thought came to me that I should take a mop and brush and go to work on it, but I couldn't. At least I didn't. I had never cleaned out a bathroom after a lot of people, and it didn't seem proper work for a man. One morning as I came in, I met Steve in the hall. He was holding a can of Dutch Cleanser in one hand and a bucket in the other. "Hi," I greeted him. "Been washing the car?"

He smiled, "Nope," and went on into his office.

When I stepped into the bathroom, it was so clean it glistened: sink, mirror, toilet, floor—everything shone. I knew that Steve had done it, the man who had given more to the community than all the rest of us put together. Steve, who had been born with a silver spoon in his mouth, hadn't considered cleaning a toilet beneath his dignity. That glistening bathroom spoke to my heart with convicting power. I cried out, "Forgive me, Lord. I've been considering myself too manly to clean bathrooms, but Steve is the real man." I was so chastened that I determined to take my turn no matter how personally revolting it was to me.

In addition to our communal apartment house, our pooled resources helped us found a New Testament church on the second floor of a Times Square storefront. I wrote my father another one of my letters:

Dear Dad,

If you can ever get up to New York, I have something so scriptural to show you that you won't believe it.

A few of us have started a church in downtown New York that will take you right back to the Christians of Ephesus and Antioch. I know that this is what Christ wants of us today, not staid ritual when we worship, but openness to the Spirit of God.

You may have been right when you said Foreign Trade Corporation wasn't the way to reach people for Christ, but this New Testament church is the way. Believe me when I tell you that all of New York City will feel its impact. God has told us through tongues and interpretation that He is making Ralph His prophet to New York, and that He has called us to hold up the prophet's arms. I have been ordained a deacon, and God says if I'm faithful, I may someday become an elder like Ralph and Bob and George.

Dad, come and see for yourself. Our services are just as Saint Paul instructed. There is prayer, prophecy, tongues and interpretation, healing and deliverance. I know you'll love it. It could add a new dimension to your life.

His reply wasn't long in coming.

Dear Harald,

No, I do not share your enthusiasm. No, I do not believe that this is what Christ wants today. No, I would not love it. Nor do I think that an ordained Lutheran minister with eight years of advanced education should be serving as deacon under elders who have had a high school education and a year or two of Bible school, if that.

Harald, it grieves my heart more than I can tell you to see my dear son persist in breaking the ordination vows he so solemnly made at the altar of Central Lutheran Church.

I tucked his letter in the back of the drawer. I had thought that if his reply was negative, I would be prepared for it and therefore unhurt. But the disappointment that welled up within me made me realize how desperately I still wanted his approval and support.

Another disappointment was right around the corner. One Sunday in our second-floor chapel, we had a visitor from Stony Brook, Long Island—a neighbor, it turned out, of Jane and

Peter. "What a saint Peter is," she glowed. "They're so happy together and make such a beautiful team."

"How nice," I responded weakly. "Um, how does Peter look?"

"The picture of health. Why do you ask?"

"Just wondering."

*He* looks *well,* I consoled myself, *but life at best is uncertain ... especially if you are married to someone intended for someone else. How fortunate that Peter is such a saint; when the Lord calls him home, he'll be ready to go.* In the words of Saint Paul, I agreed that for Peter "to depart and be with Christ was far better"—better for Peter, better for Jane, better for me.

Then, a week later, something occurred that torpedoed all my hopes that Jane would ever be my wife.

In our church was a flaxen-haired, doe-eyed young woman named Grace. She was one of the sweetest and most glowing Christians I had ever met. I always looked forward to seeing her. This particular Sunday morning, for no reason at all, I started to kneel at the communion rail beside her. Then I noticed an elderly woman heading for the same spot, so I backed away and knelt at the end of the rail.

After the service, Grace came to the back of the church. She was a shy girl who always lowered her eyes when she spoke. "Harald, I'd like to talk to you."

"Certainly." I motioned to the back pew, and we sat down.

She lifted her eyes; her shyness left her, and she was radiant. "Harald, I knew you wanted to kneel beside me at the communion rail. You were just shy, weren't you? But, Harald, you needn't be. We really are for each other. The Lord has shown me, and when you look at me, I can see in your eyes you know it, too!"

For a moment I couldn't reply. She wasn't a forward girl, and no one could be more sincere. I had to tell her the truth, but ever so gently... "Your fellowship has always meant a great deal to me, Grace, and I do love you ... like a sister." As I said the words, something nudged my memory: That was how Jane had put it, long years ago.

She raised her eyes for a moment. I saw in them the same bewildered embarrassment that I knew so well from experience. She backed out of the pew, turned and nearly ran out the door.

That night, before the evening service, she was her own radiant self again. When I saw her I thought, "Well, that heartbreak mended fast!" She came across the church to me and said, "You can imagine how I felt this morning when you told me you loved me only as a sister. I had been so sure of God's leading. I went home and prayed, 'Lord, what is the meaning of this?' I thought maybe He would speak to me through His Word. I opened the Bible and let my finger fall on a verse—" and then, triumphantly, "this is what He gave me!"

She handed me her Bible, pointing to the verse. There it was: "Cast not away therefore your confidence which hath great recompense of reward. For ye have need of patience that, after ye have done the will of God, ye might receive the promise."

"You see!" she exclaimed. "We *are* for one another—in His time, I mean."

It was all I could do not to double over—as if someone had kicked me in the stomach. Inwardly I groaned, "Oh no! That's God's promise to *me* for *Jane,* not His promise to you for me."

But I had to face it. It could be ... it could be that both of us were misinterpreting that promise. In that moment I knew that God had not chosen Jane for me.

"Grace," I said, my voice shaking, "Grace, I don't know what to say. Can we just wait on it for a while?"

She agreed that it might be the best thing to do.

Monday, my day off, dawned bright, warm and windy. What a day for a sail! All I lacked was the boat, the girl and the mood. I went for a walk. I walked all the way out to College Point Park, a lovely promontory jutting out into lower Long Island Sound. There on a seaside slope I spent the day, alternately pacing and lying on the ground. As Southerners say, I "fussed" at God.

Face down on the grass, I told God how I felt about the way He had treated me. "How could You let me live under this illusion all these years? Why did You let me think You were giving me Jane, when all along You knew You weren't?"

From the day God had promised me Jane, I had not looked elsewhere for a wife. I had dated many girls, but none seriously. After all, if you know whom you are going to marry ... I had felt like a man betrothed.

Now at 31, I had to start again from scratch. I knew I had no time to lose, but I was plagued by doubts.

What if I should meet another girl, fall in love, and be rejected a second time?

If I did meet the right girl, how would I know it? All signs had pointed to Jane, and she had turned out to be the wrong one. How could I ever again be sure of God's will in this or any other matter?

Would I ever be able to get Jane out of my mind? What if she haunted me after I married someone else? What if, when I held my wife in my arms, I would be thinking of Jane? How unfair to my wife! How terrible for me ... for the rest of my life to be living a lie!

What if the "great recompense of reward" was a purely spiritual blessing—not Jane or even marriage, but a whole new intimacy with God, a fuller experience of what the wedding ceremony describes as the mystical union between Christ and His church, of which marriage is a symbol?

I spoke the words aloud: "The mystical union that subsists between Christ and His church."

I had attended weddings all my life, but now it was as if I was hearing the words for the first time.

Why, I wondered, did Saint Paul believe he could serve Christ best as a celibate? What did Jesus mean when He spoke of "eunuchs for the Kingdom of God's sake"?

Was this what Jesus was asking of me?

Lying there, I tried to imagine what it would be like to spend the rest of my life without a mate, without a companion, without children ... What a dismal prospect! I felt neither willing nor able to face it.

I sat up and watched a young family setting out in their sailboat. Their voices carried over the water so clearly it was easy to listen in. How eager they sounded! How happy they looked, even from a distance! It was a boat full of love and joy, and I longed to be in it.

Suddenly I saw it. This was the way it was always going to be—me looking on at other people's happiness—always a spectator, never a participant. A scene flashed before my mind—a picture from an old Victorian storybook that Grandma had read to me as a child: a family on a snowy winter's eve, basking in the warmth of a fireplace and each other's love—and outside, his nose pressed tightly against the pane, a little urchin...

"Harald," I said aloud, "that boy is you. It's the story of your life—always a spectator of other people's joy—never a participant."

Then—suddenly—unexpectedly, an amazing thing happened. God embraced me. I felt a love so great, so warm, so tender, it totally enveloped me and filled each aching emptiness.

It was as if Jesus, His arms around me, was looking full into my face and saying, "Harald, I love you, isn't that enough?"

In that instant, I knew that it was...
"Yes, Lord. If I have You—and I do have You—I have everything I really need in this life and the life to come." I closed my eyes and basked in a light that was warmer and brighter than the dazzling sun.

Then suddenly I was singing ... an old Gregorian chant I had learned in seminary. The seventh century monk who had written it was, of course, himself a celibate—and in a moment of utter loneliness he, too, must have been embraced by Love—how else could he have written the words I was chanting?

Who is there like thee
Jesus unto me?
None is like thee
None above thee
Thou art altogether lovely
None on earth have we
None in heaven but thee.

My spirits lifted—higher and higher. What a change!

I could not say with David in his psalm, "I waited patiently for the Lord." I had been anything but patient with Him—but even so, He did for me what

He did for David: "He inclined His ear unto me and heard my cry. He brought me up out of an horrible pit, out of the miry clay, and set my feet upon a rock, and established my goings. He put a new song in my mouth."

The "new song" was 12 centuries old. I went from it to another, 4 centuries old:

My merry heart is springing
And knows not how to pine
Tis full of joy and singing
And radiancy divine.
The sun whose smiles so cheer me
In Jesus Christ alone.
To have Him always near me
Is heaven itself begun.

My heart sang the lyrics over and over for days. It wasn't that I no longer desired marriage, but I accepted with my whole heart God's will for my life, even though I knew now that it did not include Jane and might not include marriage.

The problem of marriage had abated, but other problems increased. Our New Testament church was becoming more and more a burden for me. Ralph Montanus was the founder of the church, and he ruled it through prophecies, some of which I inwardly questioned—but only inwardly, as I did not want to be considered unspiritual and rebellious toward God.

I began to have more and more doubts about them. I didn't want to be disruptive or go against Scripture, yet somehow I didn't feel right about them. I thought that maybe I was just too unsurrendered and spiritually blind. I doubted and refused to doubt at the same time, until I felt absolutely torn apart inside.

One of the prophecies specifically directed that we should rent a store building and have a nursery for the children of blind parents. After we leased the store and fixed it up, the city wouldn't give us a permit. In other words, our prophecy had caught God completely unaware. The project had taken 400 dollars that actually went down the drain. I would have backed out right then, but I said to Steve, who had given so much, "I feel rotten about the way your money is being used. In fact, I feel responsible. Aren't you upset?"

"Not at all. God told me to give that money. Whatever happens to it is not my responsibility."

So even Steve was unconcerned. Maybe it was just me. I decided to do nothing. Then during the evening service one Sunday night, Ralph began to prophesy. I tried to be open to his words, but in a few moments my openness turned to alarm. We were being told to open a branch of the Gospel Association for the Mind in Canada. Even the city was named: Fredericton, New Brunswick. Also, we were to open a mission close by Fredericton in a place called Geary. At the end of the prophecy, everyone began praising the Lord that He had spoken so directly.

Ralph said, "Friends, I feel that the Lord would have George and Anna Wheeler and Harald Bredesen meet this new challenge."

"Oh, no!" My heart cried out in rejection of this plan. Could any man prophesy so accurately for another? What's more, if I left New York, I'd have to leave Foreign Trade Corporation in which I had invested so much time and money.

I agonized and called for days. "Oh, Jesus, what do You want? Is this prophecy that I doubt with all my heart right? I don't know what to do."

Everyone else in the New Testament church assumed I was going. With many misgivings, I disposed of my stock in Foreign Trade Corporation and set off for a new frontier with George and Anna Wheeler. For once, I didn't write my father a glowing letter.

Geary was a little backwoods community where everyone seemed related to everyone else. In fact, half of the people had the same last name, Carr. There was a Pentecostal church there, but it was so old, hard-line and legalistic, it repelled the young people.

We moved into a two-story rattrap of a house, absolutely stripped of furniture. Then the three of us went from room to room making a list of everything we needed to make the house livable and claimed from God every item on that list. With fireside meetings in mind, we put at the top of the list "a big potbellied stove with glassine windows all around so that everyone in the room can watch the fire inside."

George and Anna were a few years older than I, but a great deal of fun to work with. Their love for God and for people—especially young people—was beautiful to behold and irresistibly attractive to the teenagers who swarmed through the house at all hours of the day and night. Even though we couldn't provide them any furniture to sit on, we did offer them open hearts and a lot of floor space. Anna always had the coffeepot on, the cookie jar full, and her guitar ready to lead us in a song. George always knew just when to bring a word in due season. We also found a novel way of decorating the big living room where we had our meetings.

It was the fall of the year, and the forests around us were robed in all their glory. The loggers in the adjoining forest let us have their thinnings—about 50 red-leafed saplings—which we placed side by side all along the walls. Not only did they beautify the walls, but the tops bent over, festooning the entire ceiling. Suddenly that big drab living room was aglow with warmth and color. Then we all sat on the floor and laughed and sang and sang and laughed and prayed and talked about Jesus. Teenagers came to Christ by the score, until every day we had at least one new convert to praise God for. I wondered if I had ever been so happy, and praised the Lord for bringing me there.

One morning when we had been up until two the night before, we arose at our usual six o'clock hour and started praying. A prophecy came through George. "Take thy rest for two hours. And at the end of that time, I will do a thing that will astound thee."

Even though I wasn't convinced that God always spoke in King James English, the message was clear enough. We set our alarm. At the moment the alarm clock sounded, a big car towing a huge fourwheeled trailer pulled into the yard. In the trailer was everything we had specified on our list that we needed in the house, including a huge potbellied stove with see-through glassine windows all around. Unbeknownst to us, 65 miles away, some kind souls had heard of our plight and were suddenly impelled to do something about it.

Overnight, George became our prophet, and the prophecies came thick and fast. Lives were being affected, as people hung on every word. I found I was right back with the same problem I had in New York—directive prophecy, the one thing I had wanted to get away from. Here I was, living with it day in and day out.

It became more and more a burden, until one day, after we'd been there for three months, I got down on my knees and cried out, "Jesus, You said Your sheep would know Your voice. I've got to know if it is Your voice that is coming through George. Am I too unspiritual to hear that it is You, or am I the only one to see that it is not?" In my mind I heard the words, "My sheep shall know My voice." And I cried out, "Oh, Lord, I *am* one of Your sheep! I must know Your voice!" I just barely got the words out when the phone rang. It was Ralph Montanus. "Harald, we need you here. Please come at your earliest convenience." I took his call as an answer to prayer.

All the way back to the States, I pondered and prayed over the subject of prophecy. I thought of the words of Paul in 1 Thessalonians 5:20-21: "Despise not prophesyings. Prove all things; hold fast to that which is good." I saw that "Despise not prophesyings" is a direct word of command, but the words that follow, "Hold fast to that which is good," clearly imply that there will be some prophecy that will *not* be good, and that it is *not* to be held fast. I could see that we are not to despise the gift, yet we are to recognize that the channels through which it comes are imperfect. Prophecy therefore must be carefully proven and judged.

Paul must have written this because even in his day there were many people who, with perhaps the highest of motives, were using prophecy to direct other people's lives, or in some cases to prop up their own authority. Our mistake had been that none of us were carefully proving or judging before we accepted each prophecy.

And as I drove across the Canadian border, I came to see that prophecy can never be by itself directive. It may be preparational or confirmational, but never by itself directional. It may prepare me for something God is going to speak directly to my heart. It may confirm something that He has already spoken to me. But I must never let it by itself direct me.

As the skyscrapers of New York welcomed me back, I felt a great relief. It was good to be home and good to have the question of prophecy settled in my mind once and for all. That night, I forced myself to share my convictions with Ralph and discovered that he, too, had reached the same conclusion. That marked the end of directional prophecy in the New Testament Christian church. Once Ralph had realized our mistake, he was very frank in admitting it. Today I count him one of the most solid Bible teachers I know.

Upon my return to our community home, I found a letter from my dad, who had retired and was now living in Venice, Florida. I took it into my room and turned it over a couple of times in my hands before I opened it. Then I ripped the side, pulled out the letter, and read:

Dear Harald,

Your mother and I would like you to come home for a family reunion. Uncle Harold will be here, Norman is coming, and so is Aunt Lydia. We are anxious to gather our family together again.

I put the letter on the table beside my bed with a heavy heart. As good as it would be to see Mother, who was always such a defender of mine, I didn't know how I could ever return and face Uncle Harold, whom I had failed by not becoming anything close to a diplomat. How could I face Aunt Lydia, Dad's older sister, who for so many years had been president of the Women's Missionary Federation, the top position a woman could occupy in the Norwegian Lutheran Church? I was sure her main purpose in coming was to retrieve me for Lutheranism. How could I ever face Norman, who had made a fortune in the South Pacific, when I was still as poor as could be? How could I face my father when so many of his opinions about the New Testament church had been closer to the truth than mine?

I said, "Oh, Jesus, I don't want to go there and let them see I'm such a flop." He didn't answer me, but there in the silence of that little room, I knew I'd have to go home.

# 12

Since Venice, Florida, was the end of the line, I had to tote my big suitcase the entire length of that long East Coast Railroad train before I finally came to the car that was to be my home for the next 32 hours. It was 1951. The United States was at war in Korea, and by the time I plunked down into my seat, I was sure that I had passed every soldier and sailor in the U.S. Army and Navy. I leaned back and looked around. My fellow passengers seemed so young. At 33, I felt older than I had in a long while.

How long it seemed since I had been their age with all those dreams of success! As I slouched against the window and shut my eyes, a parade of memories crowded into my consciousness and marched in unorderly procession past the reviewing stand of my mind: Glenwood Lutheran Church—"Harald, lovest thou Me?" "Yes, Lord"; Warren Morno—"God lifted me from my bed and healed me"; Pastor Emmett—"Why not try Dr. Jesus first?";

Joe Belgum—"They say you'll either be the biggest success or the biggest flop in the class"; Dad—"It doesn't sound like a ministry to me"; Dr. Knapp—"Your project for a great life-of-Christ movie is too visionary to ever succeed"; New York City—"Jesus, Jesus, Your name is so sweet"; Sam Shoemaker—"If you exploit these men, you will explode them"; Abram Vereide—"You can bring these leaders to Jesus"; John Gounaris—"The Holy Ghost will empower you"; Pentecostal camp—"Jesus, I'll praise You till I drop" and "Bracia, Bracia, you call me Brother!"; Jane—"Are you running ahead of the Lord?"; Foreign Trade Corporation—"Jesus, I'll be a nobody for You"; Dad again—"When will you fulfill your broken vows?"; Gospel Association for the Blind—"This man has grandeur"; New Brunswick—"Jesus, You said Your sheep would hear Your voice"...

The memories filed on and on, through Virginia, Georgia, and on into Florida, to the outskirts of Venice, to within blocks of the home that Uncle Harold had given my parents. At the end of the parade, it occurred to me again that I was 33 years old. I wondered what I had to show for my life. I had no money, no recognition, no success. My friends were all married; I didn't even have a prospect. My only asset was that I knew and loved Jesus and believed every word He spoke was for today. Something in me asked, *Isn't thatwealth enough?* Across the station platform, I glimpsed my parents watching each slowly passing car for their son. "Yes, Lord, I *am* rich in You. But how can I make them understand?"

The train nudged so slowly to a stop that it was as if it was dreading the pain of the final halt, or perhaps I was only giving it my own mood. Then there was that last jerk and the hiss of brakes releasing air, and I knew there was no more putting it off. I stood up, grabbed my traveling bag, and strode to the doorway. Resolutely, I backtracked along the platform to where I had seen my parents.

Reaching them, I hugged and kissed Mom and then Dad (we were known as the "kissing Bredesens"). Before we reached the car, they started in on me, first Dad and then Mother, back and forth. "Son, tell me you have given up that New Testament church." "Harald, dear, it's time you make something of your life." "When are you going to come back to the Lutheran ministry?" "Oh, Harald, I weep to think of those wasted years of education." "What you call faith, son, I call irresponsibility!" "My dear sweet boy, it's still not too late. Come to your senses."

I knew I had failed to find my niche; no one knew it more painfully than I did. Didn't they know how it hurt to have them reiterate my failure—how much it hurt me to be hurting them? But on and on they went. It was not until I asked them to turn around and take me back to the train that they fell into grieved silence.

Our first stop was Uncle Harold, now retired after 30 years in Congress. He was a self-made man who, because of his build, voice and personality, reminded people of Winston Churchill. He looked down on those who had the potential to succeed and didn't. Moreover, I was his namesake, which, in his eyes, made what had happened to me all the sadder.

He greeted me from across the room, holding out his hand. But his opening sentence floored me. "How much money do you have in the bank?"

"Why none, Uncle Harold." I knew he thought it was terrible I didn't contribute to the folks' support, though even without his many gifts, they lacked nothing.

There was one Bible verse that Uncle Harold knew by heart. He fixed me with a steely-eyed gaze and in his fantastically rich, booming voice recited it: "He that provideth not for his own is worse than an infidel." Then, shaking his head, he added, "And here you used to be my favorite nephew."

In spite of myself, I smiled. For a moment I was reminded of that incident with the woman on the bus and what those two policemen would have thought if I had said, "This woman is full of demons, and I'm just casting them out!" It would have sounded weird to them, almost as weird as it would to Uncle Harold if I were to say, "My riches are in Jesus who died for me ... Jesus, the same yesterday, today and forever. I'd be only too happy to share them, not only with Mom and Dad, but with you." Instead, I said nothing. To deep-dyed Lutherans, the prerequisite for spiritual riches was membership in the Lutheran church.

On the way to my parents' home, I received the first piece of good news since my arrival: Aunt Lydia had been unable to come. So the only one left to face was Norman. Even though I no longer felt threatened by his tall, handsome shadow, or his material success, I was loath to meet him for another reason. Norman was a true financial genius and something of a desperado. During the Indonesian War for Independence, he and his partners used the surplus war vessels they had purchased from the United States government to run guns through the Dutch blockade, and after the war, they had gone into inter-island trading. He would write letters to me that said, "Arrived in Manila with $18,000, to paint the town red." I imagined him getting farther and farther from the Lord and becoming hard and slick. That was the reason I dreaded seeing him.

At my parents' home, he came across the room, arms out, ready to greet me. There was such a sincere and broken quality in his face that I was astounded. It was just like a sign from God. We hugged and kissed each other, shook hands, and clapped one another on the back for good measure. Later that week, I asked him to attend a Youth for Christ meeting. To my amazement, he said yes. That night we sat side by side in a high school gym and prayed together. When the call for decisions was made, Norman raised his hand and cried out, "Oh, God, make me a real person."

That night he told me, "The reason I went to the South Pacific and made all those deals was that I never felt I was real, and I thought if I made a lot of money I could prove myself as a person..."

As he talked, I prayed, "Oh, Jesus, forgive me for judging him hard and slick, when in reality we were both trying to do the same thing—prove ourselves." And at that moment all the envy and estrangement I had ever felt for him melted away.

Norman confessed to me that he had risked everything in one great leap, a big salvage expedition that would have made him and his two partners millionaires. To beat the competition, they had to go through the typhoon belt during the typhoon season. They gambled and lost. Their ships were wrecked in a typhoon, and they were completely wiped out.

So far Norman hadn't been able to break the news to Mom and Dad. Here in this little Florida town where they had retired, they lived in the shadow of Uncle Harold, who was the town's Mr. Big. They couldn't point with pride to me, but they did to Norman. To the whole town, he was still "the Bredesens' ship-owner son." "Of course, I do own ships." He smiled ruefully. "The only problem is, they are on a coral reef in the South Pacific."

A few mornings later, Norman came to me on the side and asked, "Harald, do you remember that money I once advanced you to get started in Foreign Trade Corporation?"

"Yes, I do, but you told me I could pay you when my ship came in. My ship never did come in."

"Do you admit a legitimate debt?"

"Certainly."

"Well, you are always talking about God supplying every need. I have to have 300 dollars in two weeks, because I must go to New York to start again from scratch. Wouldn't you call that a genuine need?"

"It is, Norman." I promised him that I would get the money for him somehow. At the end of the first week, I received a letter from a man I had helped once in New York, and in it was 30 dollars, a tenth of what Norman wanted.

Then the next week I was invited to speak at a private home in Coral Gables. It was a wealthy community, and I was sure it was God's provision for the remainder of Norman's money. There were people of many religious backgrounds there—truth seekers, metaphysicians, and everything else. I had decided to speak on my quest for truth, and how I was led to Jesus who is the Truth. I had scarcely begun when a woman interrupted, "We see you have an open mind. What do you think of spiritualism?"

"There's a definite supernatural power there; even *Life* admits that in 2 percent of the hundreds of cases that they have investigated, there is no natural explanation." I looked out across the room, and everybody was smiles. I continued, "It *is* supernatural; it is demonic. The reason Scripture calls these demons 'familiar spirits' is that they are familiar with all the details of the lives of our departed loved ones and so can impersonate them to a tee."

As I spoke, I could feel the atmosphere grow cold. I hadn't realized till then that Arthur Ford, our host, was the world's foremost spiritualist, and that the room was full of mediums. I thought, "Oh boy. There goes Norman's money." But I just hewed to the line. And as I spoke, I could feel a powerful anointing of the Lord, and I heard myself speak with His authority.

Of course, Arthur Ford had authority of a sort, too. Houdini's wife credited him with being the only medium to have actually contacted her deceased husband. It was because of his pre-eminence in his field that years later Bishop Pike chose him as the medium to contact his departed son on Canadian television. Though I realized the unlikelihood of my getting through to him, I looked into his face and saw the story of his life—moral defeat. Because he had failed to walk in the light, his light had become darkness. I felt a great compassion for him.

Afterward, a lovely couple came up to me and said, "God sent you here to warn us. We sensed spiritualism was wrong, but our only son was shot down over Korea, and we had such a yearning to communicate with him, we were willing to do even this. There is a great need for God in this state, and we're going to pray that He will keep you here." They and others presented me with a love gift coming to 270 dollars.

So Norman had his money, and I had my calling. For the next six months, my mission field would be Florida. I felt certain God was calling me to a ministry of evangelism, and I yearned to devote my full time to it. I wanted to give every moment I could to bringing others to Jesus.

I prayed about this night and day until I was sure of God's will. Even at that, the method He gave me for reaching people was so unorthodox that if it hadn't been for the marvelous harvest of souls, I could not have believed it was He who was leading me. Dressed only in a polo shirt, slacks and shoes, and carrying a briefcase, I began hitchhiking back and forth across the middle of Florida, praying that only those who were ready to know the Lord Jesus would pick me up.

I liked to get out at the edge of town and start walking, rather than stand at a corner with my thumb out. That way I could be sure it was the Holy Spirit when a car stopped. One day, I walked a long way without a ride, and I thought, "Well, I'm getting a chance to get prayed-up." By the time I had walked five miles, I was really prayed-up, and no car in sight. Then a car came barreling down the highway. The driver slammed on his brakes, and I got in. As the car picked up speed, I discovered my young driver was an accountant. "I can tell from looking at you that you could afford a ride. Why do you hitchhike?"

I grinned. "Ever hear that commercial, 'I'd walk a mile for a Camel'?"

"Sure."

"Well, I've just walked five miles for your soul."

"Huh?"

"I've been praying that no one would pick me up except the man who was ready to receive Christ."

He shook his head in wonder. "You're not going to believe this. Four days ago, we finished a two-week revival in our little Baptist church, and the last night the evangelist said, 'I've been preaching my heart out in these meetings, and if anyone goes out unsaved tonight, his blood will be on his own head.' I knew he was talking to me, and I've been haunted by his words."

Driving down the highway at 65 miles per hour, he confessed his need of Jesus and asked Him to come into his heart and take over.

Back and forth across the state I went. Every day saw marvelous conversions. I stayed in the homes of Christians if I could, or settled at the end of the day in cheap boarding houses. One morning I woke up with a maddening itch. I itched all that day. By night I had several scabs on my body, and as I scratched one, I saw it move almost imperceptibly. Suddenly it dawned on me—lice—body lice!

I scrubbed and lathered and showered that night. Too embarrassed to go to a pharmacy, I tried vinegar, rubbing alcohol, harsh laundry soap, and every other home remedy I could think of. I washed my clothes, but in a few days I was itching again. No matter what I did, it seemed I couldn't get permanently rid of the lice. I couldn't go home; if I ever brought lice into my mother's house, I knew I would never hear the end of it. I was beside myself itching in the heat. I was ill at ease in people's cars, wondering if they could guess I had lice.

One evening as I paced the tiny room where I was spending the night, the thought came to me, *Harald, you've forsaken all for Jesus and what has it gotten you—just lice! How low can you sink?* Finally I stopped pacing. I picked up my Bible and started reading. I came to the passage in Acts where Paul and Silas were thrown into prison. Certainly those cells must have been infested with every kind of vermin. Those men knew what it meant to itch with lice, but instead of just scratching and feeling sorry for themselves, they praised God and sang hymns. I closed the Bible and stood in the middle of the old boarding-house room. Raising my hands, I began praising Jesus and then I began to sing. After a few minutes, I heard a knock on the door; then it opened slightly, and the landlady peeked her head in and asked, "Is anything wrong?"

I began witnessing to her about the lice, and how I had washed and washed but couldn't get rid of them, but now, like Paul in prison, I was praising the Lord.

She threw up her hands. "Land sakes, boy! You don't gets rid of lice by praising or by washing. You gets rid of lice by killing the nits. You come with me." She took me to the kitchen and poured boiling water from two huge teakettles into a large pan. Then she dumped into the pan the most terrible-smelling disinfectant I had ever come across. "Now, young man, you take this to your room, and you wash your hair and you wash your whole self until every inch of you is so clean you squeaks. Then you take every bit of your clothes and put them by the door and get in bed. I'll come and get them clothes and see that they gets clean with this here disinfectant, and you stay in your bed until I bring them back."

I was so grateful that I did exactly what she said. When my clothes came back the next morning, they reeked of disinfectant—a small price to pay for my newfound itch-free existence.

By the time I got back to my parents' home, I had seen dozens and dozens of people come to Jesus; I had learned the value of praising God in *all* things; and—I had spent nearly every cent of what little money I had brought to Florida.

Unfortunately, the day before I returned, Aunt Lydia had called Dad.

She was the much-loved and respected matriarch of the Bredesen family, and sometimes, it seemed to me, of the whole Lutheran church. I had seen tears of joy and pride in her eyes the day I was ordained. Now her tears were of a different sort. "What's Harald doing?" she had asked. "Floundering around as usual?"

"Yes, Lydia. He believes he's called to a ministry of hitchhiking."

"And at 33," she sighed.

Dad didn't repeat what else Aunt Lydia had said, but whatever it was, by the time I arrived home, he was feeling even more than his usual distress toward my way of life. He and Mother sat me down for a heart-to-heart talk about finances. Dad spoke first. "Harald, you're down to your last five dollars. Now you say you've seen these tremendous conversions, but if these people really received Christ, they would feel some burden for you financially. Not one of them has even so much as inquired regarding your support."

I said, "You know, that's right."

Mother, who had been my defender for so long, now sided with Dad.

"Harald, we are going to insist you take a job." Back and forth they went, painting my "irresponsible way of life" in darker and darker colors.

Just then, the phone rang. Dad took it and said, "It's for you, Harald. It's Western Union." It was a wire from Abram Vereide in Washington. "Annual board meeting tomorrow afternoon. If you can appear before us, I think we can make you a salaried staff member."

Mother clasped her hands and beamed when I recited the news. "Now there's something concrete and specific!"

Dad said, "Harald, there's a plane leaving here in two hours. I'll give you the fare and put you on it myself."

I told them, "This looks like God's provision all right, especially from the timing, but I've got to be absolutely certain. Just let me go out in the backyard and pray and be sure I have God's leading." Surely I was doing what God had commanded in His word by seeking out these lost Florida souls. Also, I did have peace that this was what He wanted for me; in fact, I felt burdened to keep on doing what I was doing. But outward circumstances seemed to point in another direction. I thrust my hands in my pocket and paced back and forth, crying out loud, "Jesus, if You want me to go to Washington, why have You given me a burden for Florida? Jesus, if You really do want me to stay in Florida, why aren't You meeting my financial needs?"

I heard a voice half-shouting at me from across the fence. "Is that any way to talk to the Lord? Get your hands out of your pockets." There, watching me, was an 83-year-old man, a Mr. Bartlett, whom I hadn't noticed until that moment. He had sold Henry Ford his first factory and was now a wealthy man, as well as a devout, oldfashioned Methodist. "And why are you calling on God like that? Aren't you going to stay here in this state and continue evangelizing? Certainly the church isn't doing it."

"Well, yes, if my financial needs were met."

"What are your financial needs?"

"Twenty-five dollars a week."

"From now on you'll receive a weekly check for 25 dollars, and more if you need it. I intend to keep you in chicken feed as long as you spread the gospel in Florida. But—" he pointed his finger at me "—if you ever leave Florida, this check ceases. Then God will have another provision for you."

I thanked Jesus and then thanked him. Back in the house, I told my parents, thinking that they would marvel at God's direct intervention. Actually, their only emotion that I could tell was relief. Dad sighed, "It's not enough to support a wife, but thank God you're not going to be an object of charity." Mother, who wanted so desperately to be proud of me, said, "At least, Harald, it means there is someone who believes in you."

Back and forth I hitchhiked, and during the time I was home, I did youth work in the local high school, the Methodist church, and in the mission Dad had established in what was then called the black quarter. It was a satisfying life, but at the same time I found myself longing for a mate. Since I was convinced that I could never love anyone but Jane, it would not be fair, I thought, to marry, and I had resigned myself to a life of celibacy.

Then something occurred twice that made me wonder. Two times I was tempted to commit fornication, almost to the point of irretrievability. Each time, I promised myself, "Now I know the kind of situation to avoid, and I will."

The third episode began at a CFO camp in Florida where I had been called to be a song and youth leader. I became interested in a lovely, graceful prophetess named Leah. She was a widow of about 30, with two young sons. We met at a creative-writing session, where each of us shared what we had written. She thought my poetry was God-given. During one of the sessions, quite out of the blue, she delivered a startling prophecy about the coming of Jesus Christ. It was anointed, scriptural and beautiful, and it deeply moved me. I became fascinated with her. Before long, my fascination turned to strong attraction. We spent as much time together as possible, until I dreaded the ending of camp and leaving her.

A week after camp, I was invited to a beach party. The first person I saw, the only person I saw, was Leah. She had arranged the invitation. It was wonderful to be with her, and before we knew it, we had left the group and wandered down a lonely strip of beach. She said, "Come on, Harald. The further we get from the crowd, the more alone we can be with God."

She was wearing a filmy pink dress, and as the wind blew off the water, it clung to her and outlined the soft contours of her body. All my instincts told me that we were heading into the very kind of situation I had determined to avoid, but we continued walking. We stopped once and took off our shoes. Then, holding hands, we walked barefoot out along the spit, a long low island of sand dunes. It was lonely and private, and the wind kept blowing around us as we walked. Behind us, as we sat down, was a dune. In front of us was only the immense expanse of the Atlantic.

I took off my shirt, and we leaned back on it. I knew how wrong it was. I wanted to say, "Let's get up and start back." I began, "Leah—"

"Yes, Harald," she breathed, in a dreamy seductive whisper. And I couldn't say it. Satan came to me in that moment and said, "As long as you're going to be celibate for the rest of your life, you should at least know what you're giving up for the Lord." And in the heat of the moment I agreed with him. "Yes, I should have just one bite of this cake before I surrender it all." I put my arm around Leah and drew her close, and she nestled her head on my bare chest. Our breathing became as one, and quickened.

Then Leah sat up and prayed, "For what we are about to do, forgive us, O Lord."

I burst out laughing. All of a sudden I saw how ludicrous Satan's temptation was. To top it all, just then a surf fisherman came over the dune behind us and nearly stumbled over us. He smiled. "It's a lovely place to take your wife."

I was so embarrassed by his intrusion that the fever for Leah left me just as abruptly as it had come. I grabbed my shirt, pulled Leah to her feet, and together we started back. All the way back I praised Jesus aloud that He had saved me from my own stupidity. It was by no means *my* victory, but the sovereign intervention of God. I thought of the words of the psalmist: "Truly God is good to Israel, but as for me, my feet were almost gone, my steps had well nigh slipped ... so foolish was I and ignorant; I was as a beast before thee."

Shortly after that, I confided what had happened to Hal Miller, who occupied my parents' upper-floor apartment and had been like a member of our family—my closest Florida friend and only confidant. "Don't you see, Harald? Leah may have felt God had chosen you to be her husband and the father of her two sons, and she was just helping Him along a bit. You would have spent the rest of your life trapped by your own stupidity."

I never heard from Leah again, but the enemy wasn't going to let me forget my near slip with her. He tempted me, not with lust, but in a more subtle way. He soon had me wallowing in a slough of self-recrimination. "A fine man of God you are! Who are you to lead souls to

Christ when you are so far from Him yourself that you could fall into such a trap?"

I would pray and resist Satan. The thoughts would leave. Then, when I was least expecting them, the enemy would assail me again. One day I was getting ready to phone a fellow by the name of Doug Bell, a man of about 45 who worshiped at the shrine of success. He was a New York broker who had made so much money that he had been able to retire to Florida and spend his time deep-sea fishing on his yacht. At that very moment, I knew he was on his boat awaiting my call to tell him when I could go deep-sea fishing with him—not knowing that I was angling for his soul. As I looked up his number, the accusations came back, so strong, so forcibly, I nearly buckled under them.

I began to agree. "Who am I to think I can win this man for Christ? Look at the sin in my life. Look what an adulterer I am, for the Bible says that he who looks upon a woman to lust after her has already committed adultery with her in his heart." The more I berated myself, the more reluctant I grew to pick up the phone.

Not wanting to at all, I took the receiver and forced myself to dial the marine telephone operator in Sarasota, and when Doug came on the line, we set a date.

On the day we had picked, the Lord provided a torrential downpour, so we spent the day in his guesthouse where I was quartered and studied the Bible together. Somewhere in the book of Romans, he knelt down and received Jesus as his Savior. It was a good lesson to me that yesterday's sins should never keep us from doing what God would have us do today.

One of the encouraging developments while I was in Florida was that though Uncle Harold never did accept my way of life, he was impressed with the response I was getting in the local high school where I had started a Christian youth club; and the second month I was there, he invited me to use his new home on the Gulf during his many trips to Washington. A frequent guest and regular bridge partner of his was Mrs.

Forbes, the widow of the chairman of a Wall Street bank. One evening, when I called on her, she introduced me to her guest, Edna Lovely, the widow of a partner of a famed meat-packer.

Mrs. Lovely was a striking grand dame with all of the bearing of American and European high society. As soon as we were introduced, I began talking about Jesus in my usual head-on approach. As I talked, she almost leaped forward in her chair, and right before the horrified eyes of Mrs. Forbes, knelt down and asked Jesus to come into her heart. A few nights later, she woke up speaking in tongues. Never had I seen a socialite come to Jesus so fast, and I couldn't help being curious as to what had so dramatically prepared her heart.

One night she told me. "I'm going to tell you something I have never told another soul. For years and years I've yearned for spiritual truth. I couldn't find it in the orthodox church, nor in metaphysics, nor in the many, many other places I looked. I spent six weeks in a spiritualist camp and later studied yoga with a famous guru in India. Then one night a man appeared who was visible only to me. He said he was a prince from the court of Cleopatra. He was as real as you are. At first I was fascinated by him. Then he began to assert a power over me that put me absolutely under his control. He commanded me to do things that would completely revolt me. I would abhor myself because of them, but I couldn't stop. I couldn't explain him to a psychiatrist, for he would have had me committed, and I could hardly tell my friends. Shortly before you came, I cried out to God to help me. Then you came and began talking about Jesus, and how He sets us free from anything that binds us. That's why I was so eager to receive Him. I needed Him so much."

I praised Jesus far into the night that He had delivered Edna Lovely and that He had let me be His instrument.

One day shortly after that, a beautiful new Deluxe Plymouth station wagon was delivered to me with a substantial check for maintenance. With it was a note that said, "I want you to know that there are absolutely no strings attached to this gift. You can leave for Timbuktu with it. You have no obligation to me. I'm only doing what God told me to do." The note was signed, "Edna Lovely."

I was overwhelmed and wondered out loud to Hal if I should accept it. He laughed. "For Edna Lovely to give a car is like an office worker putting small change in a collection." I called and thanked her for her gift, and she was as nonchalant as if I had thanked her for a ride to the store. Before she hung up, she asked me to keep her in mind if I ever came across an attractive investment.

Now I had a car and could get about more easily. The summer of 1952, when I was again invited to be a song leader at various CFO camps, I accepted. One of them was at Elim Bible Institute, Lima, New York, where my dear friend Carlton Spencer was president. My roommate there was a debonair, handsome and darkcomplexioned man by the name of David Weiss.

His name had such a familiar ring to it that I asked him, "What kind of work are you in?"

"I'm kind of between jobs; you see, I just got out of Leavenworth..." He told me the story of his time in the underworld and his decision for Christ. When he mentioned his lawyer, Willis Rice, it clicked with me where I had heard the name David Weiss before.

Back at the Gospel Association for the Blind, Willis Rice had come to me and said, "I've been pleading the case of an underworld character as a means of reaching him for Christ, and I feel that you are the one who could win him." But as he talked, I had felt no witness in my heart, and so I had said, "I don't believe your David Weiss is ready for Christ yet," and dismissed it from my mind.

So here he was as my roommate. I thought, *What a coincidence. Isn't it marvelous the way the Lord arranges things and overrules our mistakes?* Because I felt sorry that I hadn't taken time with him when his attorney had first asked me to, I tried hard to make up for it by giving him all the fellowship I could during those two weeks we were roommates. One thing that bothered me about him, though, was the way he gave his testimony to my young people. It was 95 percent his past sin and only 5 percent what Jesus had done for him. Still, he was a fascinating person with a real gift of gab, and we soon became good friends.

One day during the camp, we went for a walk. "Harald, I have an invention for you, if you would like to invest in it. It's called Sani-dump; it's a brand-new idea in garbage-disposal units. There's a large company that wants to take it over, but then all the profits would be lost to the Lord." He enthused about it until I began to see that it was indeed a unique and wonderful invention. He added, "I want Christians to have the benefit of this. I want to live for God now. Would you know of any Christian who might become interested in investing?"

That very moment, up the walk came Edna Lovely. Here again was another of God's marvelous coincidences. She enthusiastically agreed to put 5,000 dollars into Sani-dump. I asked other Spirit-filled people, some of whom were at the camp, to invest also. Even my parents put in 3,500 dollars, until altogether we had 15,000 dollars.

We decided to begin manufacturing in New York. Dave found a factory that had been condemned because of plans to expand the Queensboro Bridge. The city was holding it unoccupied until they were ready to begin the new construction. A city official whom Dave knew gave us permission to use the factory during the interim. The rent was extremely low.

I was almost certain Dave had greased his palm, but when I shared my concern with the others involved, they excused him, saying, "He's a new Christian, and we mustn't expect from him what we would from a mature Christian. And after all, the city wasn't using the building." This allowed me to ease my conscience to the degree that I did not take action. Once again I was to pay an awful price for letting myself think that as long as I had protested a wrong and washed my hands of it, I could escape the guilt of it. Would I ever learn that it doesn't work that way?

Dave was constantly driving the pride and joy of my life, the new station wagon from Edna Lovely. He put several thousand miles on it each month, and it grieved me to see it wearing out so fast. I mentioned this to him as we were driving down the street one day, and he said, "Yes, Harald, I've already thought of that, and we don't want to postpone a solution." He put on the brakes, stopped by a Woolworth store, went in, and a moment later came out with a note form. He drew up and signed a promissory note for 2,700 dollars for the car. He had put so much mileage on it I was quite willing to take the note, thinking that when it came due I would buy another car.

Then one morning we found the books of the company were missing, and so was Dave. I looked for him, calling everywhere I could think of, refusing to consider the possibility that he could have absconded. Of course, my parents were again beside themselves over my foolheadedness. Dad blamed me. "So this is Harald's Holy Spirit guidance. I don't think much of it." I felt terrible that they had been duped because of me. Also, I felt terrible for my Spirit-filled friends who had invested so much.

It was the most painful lesson I could ever have on how untrustworthy coincidences are. The coincidence that my roommate should be the very person I'd already heard about, the coincidence that Edna Lovely should come up the walk just as he was asking me for money, all meant nothing. It was also a very painful lesson on how careful one must be to heed the checks of the Spirit, no matter how small and gentle. My misgivings regarding the lack of Jesus-centeredness in David's testimony and regarding his palmgreasing had been definite checks of the Holy Spirit, which I, with the help of my friends, had rationalized, to our great pain and loss.

I cried out to God and asked forgiveness for my heedlessness. Once again He was showing me through terrible suffering and humiliation that He is a Holy God who cannot bless moral compromise in any form or degree. When I worked outside of His will, I could never achieve anything but grief and injury. I received a letter from one of our investors, a Mrs. Newman: "Harald, don't berate yourself any further for having been the instrument of our investment. Jesus Christ must be head. This means *we* must be beheaded, and none of us must feel any bitterness against the instrument He uses to accomplish this." Her letter was a comfort. When I returned to Florida, I wasn't bitter, but I felt older and wiser than anyone should ever feel at the age of 34.

To plunge me down a little deeper, my parents decided it was time for another talk. Mother approached the subject first. "We believe for your own good, Harald, that you should try to find a wife. You're like a kite without a tail, soaring into the sky in one moment and falling to the ground the next. A wife would help to keep you steady. And besides, your way of life—doing whatever you want to do—is so selfish that you're going to be terrible husband material if you don't settle down soon."

Dad took a different tack. "There are still plenty of fish in the ocean,

Harald, but the bait is getting stale. If you don't marry now, while you still have some youthful appeal, you're going to end up a rootless, footloose drifter."

I could hardly answer them. They couldn't even guess the growing hunger in my own heart for a wife and the indecision that weighed so heavily because I wasn't sure if marriage was a part of God's plan for my life.

# 13

Mother paused in the doorway, looking with a puzzled frown at the morning mail in her hand. "Ever hear of Pine Bluff, Arkansas?"

"No, I don't think I ever have. Why?"

"Here's a letter for you from some woman there, a Mrs. Cora Wilson Stewart."

The message was handwritten on blue stationery, and I read it aloud.

Dear Rev. Bredesen,

I am blind and live a somewhat solitary life which gives me much time for prayer. God spoke to me that you were to come to Pine Bluff to minister to the people here. Please pray about it. I will be in touch with you shortly.

Your servant in Jesus,

Cora Wilson Stewart

Mother was aghast. "My word, Harald. How can a perfect stranger expect you to drop everything and run off to some unknown place at the drop of a hat? You're certainly not going off on this wild-goose chase, are you?"

"No, Mother, I don't think you'll have to worry about this one. I don't feel any pull at all to Pine Bluff, Arkansas."

However, I did pray about Mrs. Stewart's letter, and whenever I brought the matter to Jesus, I received a deep inner peace that witnessed to me that perhaps God *did* intend for me to leave Florida and go there. The Scripture that kept coming to mind was Acts 16:9: "And a vision appeared to Paul in the night; there stood a man of Macedonia, and prayed him, saying, Come over into Macedonia, and help us."

A week later I received a wire from Mrs. Stewart: "Dear Reverend Bredesen: Please come now."

I handed the wire to Mother, knowing that I was to go. She was dumbfounded. "Harald, this is crazy. How will you live? Mrs. Stewart doesn't mention room or board or salary or even a specific job. You're being foolhardy."

"Look, Mother, I have 50 dollars to start with, and if God really spoke to Mrs. Stewart, He'll supply what I need."

"But what if He didn't? What if her 'guidance' is only the imaginings of an old woman?"

"Well, Mother, I'm hardly signing up for life. If when I get there, God doesn't confirm that it was He who summoned me, I'm certainly not going to stay."

Throughout all this, Dad had remained uncharacteristically quiet. Now he reached across the table and patted Mother's arm. "You should know by now that Harald is going to do what he wants to do no matter what anyone says." Then he looked at me and held out his hand. "Godspeed, son." Despite his blessing, I could read the reproach in his eyes; it was as if he were saying once more, "It doesn't sound like a ministry to me."

As I drew near the city, I began looking for pines and bluffs. I saw neither. I did see a muddy, meandering stream over which I crossed into a typical Midwestern county seat of 43,000 people, with the usual "Main

Street," courthouse, and a number of small industries, the largest of which was a bauxite mill.

I moved into a square, white-frame, six-story hotel known as the White House. The only thing it had in common with its distinguished namesake was its color. But it was clean and cheap. The manager was an enormous buxom woman named Mary, who had a way of leaning over the hotel desk that left little to the imagination. I chose the hotel because, despite its manager, it seemed respectable, and also like something that I could afford.

Just as Mother had predicted, Mrs. Stewart had no idea how I was to go about ministering to the people of Pine Bluff. She only knew that God wanted me there, and her conviction was convincing. Still, there were no speaking engagements, no job, no definite course of action, and every day my money went down, down, down, like dew before the early Arkansas sun.

When I had only 10 dollars left to my name, I started getting scared. Here I was in a strange city with no friends. Mrs. Stewart was no help. She believed that God had brought me and that He would take care of me. It was the kind of faith I'd come with but was losing rapidly. What was I going to do in Pine Bluff when my money ran out?

I prayed aloud in my room, "I want to trust You, Jesus, but—" As soon as I found myself saying the word "but," I was ashamed. I knew I didn't trust Jesus, not really, not when everything was so unknown. Hoping that He would take care of me was the best I could do. I groaned and cried aloud each day for help. My only comfort was the Scripture I had taped and now played over and over all night long on my recorder.

Finally, I was completely out of money, and I went through all my pockets looking for small change. My search netted me three pennies. I lined them up in a row on top of the dresser and crawled into bed. As I was lying there in that lonely little room, the realization came down on me: "I'm utterly helpless. I have no provision for tomorrow. God is all I have. He will either prove Himself and vindicate my coming here, or I'll be dead from starvation in 40 days, the amount of time a man can go without eating."

When I realized that now God was going to *have* to show His hand, such a hilarious spirit came over me that I began to laugh and then praise God. It wasn't trust, but at least I was going to find out for sure if He wanted me here. I slept soundly for the first time since my arrival and woke up feeling like a million dollars. I walked into the hotel dining room and said, "Two eggs, two pieces of toast, and a glass of milk, please."

When I was finished, I remembered that I only had three cents. I thought, *Well, what shall I do? How is God going to work? Shall I sit here and wait for someone to drop the 25 cents I need on the table? Shall I admit to the cashier that I have no money and face the consequences?* As I sat there, the dining room began emptying, and nothing happened. All of a sudden, I couldn't wait any longer on God.

I jumped up, rushed past the cashier, saying, "Hold on a moment. I just remembered something," pretending I had an urgent telephone call to make.

In my rush, I nearly bumped into Mary's mother as she came through the door, a sweet grandmotherly woman of about 65. She put her hand on my arm. "Harald, last night in prayer God told me I was to begin giving you something out of my tithes." She handed me five dollars.

*"Praise God!"*

At the end of the day, realizing that I still had 3 dollars left over, I laughed aloud. "Just think: from 3 cents to 3 dollars in just 24 hours. That's a hundredfold capital gain. At this rate I'll soon be a millionaire."

Then I prayed, "Jesus, I thank You for providing my daily bread, but please give me outstanding proof so that I'll know within 10 days whether You called me here or not." The next day I went down to the lobby, and the manager said, "Harald, Mr. Bradford, the owner of our hotel chain, is in town, and he wants you to have lunch with him." Mr. Bradford was a wrinkled old fellow with a thatch of unruly white hair. He twisted his diamond stickpin as he talked.

He had been tormented for nearly half a century over an incident of violence that had occurred when Pine Bluff was just a frontier town. When he was through with what amounted to a life confession, he leaned toward me, his face a picture of agony. "Is there any hope for an old reprobate like me?"

I told him of Jesus and the Blood that cleanses. Together in a private room, we studied what the Bible says about salvation. "Salvation is a gift, Mr. Bradford. It has already been paid for by Jesus on the cross. It's yours for the asking."

"What about the terrible thing I did?"

"Jesus bore that and all your other sins on the cross, and now He says in His Word He's knocking on the door of your heart."

I could see it was painful for him, but he got down on his knees. Tears filled his eyes, and he spoke in a trembling old voice. "I'm sorry, Jesus. Please forgive me. Come into my heart and take over."

He knelt for a long time, and when he got up, he didn't seem to know whether to laugh or cry. I'd never seen a man so happy.

Together we went out into the lobby, and he announced with great enthusiasm to a passerby, "I've just received Jesus Christ!" He pulled out his wallet, which was thick with 100-dollar bills, and started peeling them off. "Here, Harald, I want to—"

The devil was saying to me, "Let him give them to you. He will get a blessing." But I knew if I took it, it would give him the idea that salvation was really not a free gift, so I said, "You can't pay for this. It was paid for 2,000 years ago on the cross." With all the selfcontrol I could muster, I turned away from him and his laden wallet and walked with heavy feet down the hall.

He followed me. "Okay. But from now on, you'll be a guest in my hotel."

Back in my room, I rejoiced. "Thank You, Jesus! What a confirmation that it *was* You who brought me to Pine Bluff!"

At the suggestion of Mrs. Stewart, I began to minister at the state reform school. It was notorious for its former superintendents and terrible conditions. The governor had sent in a new man who was supposed to change this situation. I preached there on a Sunday and taught the Word. After a few weeks, the paper ran a picture of me passing out Bibles and carried an editorial saying, "We need more men like Harald Bredesen."

The new superintendent of the reform school, Joe, said to me, "Harald, when you came here, you had three strikes against you."

"What were those?"

"One, two and three: You're from New York, and we're suspicious of New Yorkers."

"What do you think of me now?"

"You're okay."

I thought, *Now that I have his confidence, I can deal with him regardinghis need of Jesus.* I asked him, "Supposing you found yourself outside the gate of heaven, and Saint Peter asked, 'What makes you think we'll let you through?' What would you say?"

He wasn't one bit offended. "Well, I guess I can best answer that question in terms of a poem." And he recited a ballad about a man named Abou Ben Adhem, who saw a recording angel writing down the names of those who loved the Lord. Abou's name was not on the list, but he pointed out that he loved his fellowmen. The next night the angel returned, and Abou's name was at the top of the list. Joe said, "That's why they'd let me in. I love my fellowman."

"You're wrong, Joe. Dead wrong. And so is that poem. You're under a curse." I opened my Bible and showed him Galatians 3:10: "Those who depend on obeying the law (for their salvation) are under a curse. Salvation is a gift we have to accept, but we cannot earn." From that day on, even though I hit it off with the boys, Joe avoided me at every turn.

At the hotel I brought the message of salvation to two African-American maids. Unlike Joe, they got down on their knees and received Jesus with glad hearts.

I decided that perhaps God had put me in this hotel for another reason and that I was supposed to bring the Good News to Mary, the buxom manager. With my usual tact, I asked her my favorite question: "Mary, suppose you found yourself outside the gate of heaven...?"

She said, "Well, I'd just tick off some of the things I've done to make this a better world."

As I had done with Joe, I came down hard on her, showing her how wrong she was. My spirit was more zealous than loving. I know that now, but it took a long time to learn.

She flushed and grew angry. Pointing a finger at a drunk staggering through the lobby, she sneered, "Why waste time on me? Go to work on him. He's the hopeless one."

"On the contrary, he's the most hopeful person in this hotel. He knows he's lost and needs help. But you, Mary, you're respected in the community, so you don't realize how desperate your condition is."

"Hampff!" She was as angry as Joe, and she turned up her nose and walked away. From then on, she didn't know what to do when she saw me. Sometimes she'd give me a big crocodile smile, and sometimes she'd turn her back on me. But it was never easy for either of us.

Day in and day out, I kept my eyes open for new people to bring to Jesus. I'd walk down the streets of Pine Bluff and pray that God would lead me to a man who was ready to receive Him. It was early one morning when I saw a man of about 50 coming toward me. I felt led to talk to him. Stopping him, I said, "Sir, I'd like to talk to you about the Lord Jesus." He beamed. "I'm an elder in the Lutheran church, the one on the next block."

I pointed out to him, as I already had to several other elders in Pine Bluff churches, that if he was relying on anyone but Jesus, he was lost and in need of salvation. The man was really convicted. "Yes, yes. I know you're right. I've been relying on my church membership and my good works instead of just Jesus alone. What you're saying is true. I really must rely on Jesus and Him alone. Thank you. Thank you."

We prayed together and I left. I learned later that the moment we parted, he went into the pastor's office and shared our talk. The pastor didn't take too kindly to some outside, self-appointed shepherd ministering to the sheep of his pasture.

About this time, despite my many failures in soul-winning, Satan was sufficiently upset by my activities to try to put an end to my ministry once and for all. While I was seeking out men to bring to Jesus, unknown to me, the Lutheran pastor wrote to church headquarters and said, "There's a man here who calls himself a Lutheran minister, and his very presence is an embarrassment to me."

The director of the reform school, still furious with me, began to spread indirect but damaging rumors. "Why do you suppose Harald Bredesen is coming out here? No one asked him to come, and he's not getting paid for it. He's unmarried, and he's making friends with these boys. What do you suppose his motives are?"

And Mary told several people that she had it on good authority that Harald, despite his pious front, was bedding down with a whore. She also reported that night after night she had heard coming from my room the low hum of a radio transmitter.

Someone else reported that they had seen me talking to the maids in the hallway.

Pine Bluff was not that big a town, and it wasn't long before rumor chased rumor, until I was a regular Mr. Hyde in clericals. All of which, of course, I was oblivious to, as I went about, praying and witnessing. I did notice, however, that some people looked at me in a rather peculiar way.

Then I discovered that someone had been through my files, and soon the report was out that he had found evidence that I had a large bank account in New York City. The favorite theory in the community was that the Communists had sent me to Pine Bluff to stir up trouble among the "Negroes." In fact, I was "seen" consorting with a black woman and was "heard" sending out secret messages at night to my Communist bosses in New York.

By this time, I could see that people were becoming hostile, turning their backs and not meeting my eyes, but it didn't bother me. Not even Mary's peculiar behavior bothered me. So, I was totally unprepared for the message that was waiting for me at the hotel desk. "Mr. Bredesen, you are requested to appear before the Ministerial Council tomorrow at nine o'clock to explain your presence in this town." What had I done? All that night I wondered. I had led a few people to Jesus. I had preached at the reform school on Sundays and had led Bible studies with the boys. That was all.

The next morning I stood before the grim faces of the Council, and there, with mounting horror, realized that they actually believed the rumors. "Harald Bredesen, the following charges have been made against you: There are reports that you are having drinking and poker parties in your hotel room and have entertained a woman of ill repute. There is evidence that you have Communist sponsors in New York for whom you are agitating and to whom you are sending secret radio messages. You are undermining the leaders of our local church. And you are doing all this under the guise of being a minister."

As I listened to their charges, I felt the heat of anger rising from my legs, through my body, into my chest, and then into my head until I thought I would explode. My fingers gripped the edge of the chair. I blurted, "It's a lie! Every bit of it!"

The chairman said, "We have firsthand information from the manager of the hotel where you live and the superintendent of the reform school where you work. There is so much evidence that our local daily has assigned a reporter to uncover you. Our advice to you is, leave town immediately."

I tried to defend myself, but their minds were made up, and I could see it was hopeless. In every way they could, they made it clear that the sooner I departed the scene, the better they would like it.

Back at the hotel, there was a note saying, "Mr. Bredesen, you are no longer welcome at the school." So for days I went out in the woods, pacing back and forth until I had worn a path in the ground, crying out to God, mostly in tongues. It was the blessed release of tongues that saved my sanity. I also prayed is English, or should I say, lamented.

"Oh Jesus, why did You bring me here? My reputation is completely ruined. Oh, Jesus, what's the use of staying? No one will listen to me now. I want to leave. I want to get out of here. I want to die."

Jesus spoke definitely to me. *Satan, the father of liars, the accuser of the brethren, wants to destroy your witness for Me. If you run away in the face of his attack, you will play into his hands. It will be a confirmation of everything his servants have said about you. My son, I am putting you through a school. If you leave before you learn what I am trying to teach you, I shall have to put you through it all over again somewhere else.*

Then the Word of God came to mind from 2 Chronicles 20: "The enemy shall come up against thee ... but be not afraid, the battle is not thine but mine, saith the Lord, *stand still* and see the salvation of the Lord."

"Yes, Lord." It was the hardest yes I had ever spoken. "If You want me to, I'll stay."

Each day seemed harder than the one before, and there was no one to turn to. Jesus was all I had. Even though there was comfort in His words, they didn't erase the horrible humiliation. It was getting worse and worse to be in Pine Bluff.

I was sitting alone in my room one morning when Mary came storming in. "Mr. Bradford says you should start paying for your room. There's nothing special about you."

"Well, I'm willing to pay. I never asked to have it free in the first place. I have just one question, Mary. Is this Mr. Bradford's idea or is it yours?"

"If you really want to know, it's mine. But you can't stay here. You called this hotel a house of assignation." With that she walked out, slamming the door behind her, with all the force of her 180 pounds.

I didn't even know what a house of assignation was. But I could imagine from the sound of her voice that it was a house of prostitution. "Oh no," I thought. "So *that's* the reason she has this bitter antagonism for me. I'll just have to straighten it out and tell her I never even thought such a thing." I went down to the hotel dining room.

There was Mary, sitting on a stool behind the cash register. I went right up to her.

"Mary, I've been wondering why you were so bitterly hostile to me, and I just want you to know that I never did call this a house of assignation."

"If you're a Christian," she snorted, "I don't want anything to do with Christianity!" And then she shouted, "You get out of here!"

It was noon. The room was full of people, and every eye was on me. I hated to run from a woman, even if she was a foot taller. So I just stood my ground. "Mary, let me talk to you."

She came out from behind the cash register and, as mad as a bull, bellowed, *"You get out of here!"* In the presence of everyone, she picked me up bodily and heaved me into the lobby.

Nothing, nothing in the world ever prepared me for that moment. It was a moment of total humiliation and degradation. I got to my feet and stumbled to my room.

The two maids I had led to Jesus knocked on the door. "We just want to say, Reverend Bredesen, we don't go along with that awful woman."

I motioned them in. "Let's pray for her together."

Later, I heard that they told their mother, "Reverend Bredesen must be in the right to take it like he did."

Whether it was because of them or not, I'll never know for sure, but two days later Mr. Bradford came to see me with tears in his eyes. "I've just found out that Mary has been conducting a house of assignation here in my hotel, and her mother was the madam. I apologize for what she said about you, and I want you to know that I don't believe a word of it."

So Mary really *did* have a house of assignation. That explained why she was so anxious to ruin me, but why had her mother given me her tithe? Mr. Bradford's real estate agent had the explanation. "She gave you the money to make you think that she was a woman of prayer so that you wouldn't be suspicious. And as for Mary, when you approached her with the words of salvation, she must have thought you had caught on to her. So naturally, she wanted to have you run out of town before you could expose her."

Mr. Bradford fired Mary that day, and the story spread as rapidly through Pine Bluff as the rumors once had spread about me.

In a few more days, a banner-headline story broke out in the paper about the sadistic acts of Joe, the new superintendent of the reform school. He admitted to many things, among them that he couldn't help himself once he started whipping a boy; he couldn't stop until he saw the blood run. In response to public petition, the governor removed him.

So the whole town knew the character of the two who had been vilifying me. My reputation had been restored. Suddenly everyone was so friendly, I found myself wanting to stay in Pine Bluff.

I prayed, "Jesus, You said I had a lesson to learn. What really was accomplished in this long, horrible year?" Then He made me know that through this experience He had taught me a lesson that would help me the rest of my life: that no matter what happened, as long as I was in the clear, I could trust Him to redeem my good name. He might let it be dragged in the mud, just as His was, but He would not leave it there.

In the eyes of Mother and Dad the whole experience had been a wild-goose chase; it hadn't been any kind of ministry one could point to with pride. But for me, it had been a turning point. I knew I would always look back on Pine Bluff as the place where I learned to take literally the words of Christ in Matthew 5:11-12: "Blessed are ye *when* [not *if]* men shall revile you and persecute you and shall say *all* manner of evil against you falsely for my sake. Rejoice and be exceeding glad ... for so persecuted they the prophets which were before you."

# 14

I moved out of the hotel into an ancient, white-pillared plantation house. It was extremely run down, but soon, with the help of friends and 15 gallons of paint, I had restored it to something of its original beauty. We even managed to scrounge around for enough old furniture to furnish the top floor where I lived. I sublet the first floor. I'd been working on the place a month when Ralph Montanus called, urging me to come to Memphis to help him with a National Conference for Blind Workers.

I went, and at the end of the conference he said, "Harald, why don't you come back to the Gospel Association and do public relations work for us? We are a 30,000-dollar-a-year organization now, and we need your talents."

"Has God shown you what salary you're to pay me?"

"Harald, I know you'd come for nothing, if you thought it was God."

"If I believed it was God, I'd pay for the privilege of working with you.

But I want to see how much faith you've got that He really wants me on your team again."

"How about 25 dollars a week?" He turned to Mama Looft who had come down with him from College Point. Steve Hart and I had roomed with her our first year in College Point. "You'd take him back for 15 a week, wouldn't you? That would leave him 10 dollars a week for luxuries."

"Sure I would," she beamed.

"Well, let me pray about it," I told them.

When I did, I became convinced that this was God's next step for me. I returned to Pine Bluff with Mama Looft to gather my possessions for the long trek east. I had been able to repossess my Plymouth station wagon, which David had heavily mortgaged, and with the proceeds of its sale had purchased an old, shiny black Studebaker convertible. I had just finished loading the trunk when Cliff, my mechanic friend, came by. He stood and scratched his head. "You aren't planning to drive that heap to New York are you? Man, you're out of your mind."

No one knew that car better than Cliff, or trusted it less; he had repaired it so often. I could understand his attitude, but I did not share it. I loved that shiny old Studebaker Commander deluxe convertible. I was as hooked by it as an Arab sheikh is by his steed. So here I was, lugging out suitcases while Mama Looft, who was going to ride back with me, did last-minute packing upstairs. Cliff, seeing his pleas were falling on deaf ears, walked over and laughingly addressed himself to my car. "You'll never make it, old girl, you'll never make it. Not in a million years. Somewhere in Tennessee, they'll have to put a bullet in your engine block."

"There you go," I chided, "thinking in the natural again—just like the scoffers in Noah's day. They said his ark would never make it, but it did—to the peak of Mount Ararat. I trust, my friend, you'll recall what happened to the scoffers." With that, Cliff beat a goodnatured retreat.

I opened the door of my "ark" and proceeded to stow away my belongings. I packed and repacked, layer upon layer, higher and higher, so high, in fact, as to preclude the possibility of raising the top even in the event of rain.

Finally, everything I owned in all the world was in or on that Studebaker. Then we boarded. In that moment, it dawned on Mama that for the next few days we'd be fully exposed to the elements. The stout old lady lifted her hands toward heaven and prayed a prayer Noah never did: "Lord, don't let it rain." I uttered a prayer of my own, "Jesus, be our mechanic," and we cast off.

We must have been quite a sight, bearing down the street, the young man, now not quite so young, the beaming irrepressible old lady gleefully embarking on the greatest adventure of her 73 years, and the rakishly stacked old convertible, top-heavy as a Spanish galleon. Mama waved and smiled broadly at everyone we passed, and they waved back, smiling at least as broadly at her.

Mount Ararat was still 600 miles away when the Lord spoke to me. I wasn't asking Him for any answers, just praising Him for being our mechanic, when it came—a sudden knowing as if I'd heard a voice and yet I'd heard nothing: "You are going to be married and very soon."

"Jesus, Jesus, thank You, Jesus!" I had longed for a wife, but just how greatly, I hadn't realized until that moment. I could hardly contain my joy. I realized that God had spoken to me through what Paul in his first letter to the Corinthians calls the "word of knowledge," one of the nine supernatural gifts of the Spirit. What I now needed was a word of wisdom on how to proceed in the light of the knowledge He had given me. "Jesus, how am I going to find this girl? How will I recognize her?"

He spoke again. "You won't have to look for her. As you walk in My Spirit, I'll bring her across your path."

That word left me more excited than ever, and yet completely at rest. Since all this was going to happen very soon, and I was on my way to New York, I was sure that it would be there that I would meet her. Up until then, I had been enjoying the trip so much that I hadn't been in any hurry to reach our destination. Now, waiting for the moment our paths would meet, I was as filled with anticipation as a little child on the last long day before Christmas.

Right at noon, my first day back at the office, a radiantly lovely girl came in to go to lunch with one of the secretaries. I felt I had met her before, but I couldn't place her. I said to her, "Say, would you mind listening to this?" I was working on a script about a blind boy who falls in love with a sighted girl, and I wanted to know how the dialogue I had written would sound to a woman. She smiled yes and slipped into a chair.

As I read the script, my eyes kept leaving the page to watch her. I thought she was the most illumined, the most womanly woman I had ever seen. Whenever I had read stories as a child, I would imagine a princess who looked just like she did, except that suddenly the blonde princess had become a brunette. She had smiling brown eyes, delicate features, and a soft, pure complexion, and I could hardly take my eyes off her. There was a glowing tenderness and compassion in her face as she listened. She seemed to see everything that I was trying to get across.

Even more beautiful than her face was the sense of love and peace she exuded. I found my heart crying out, "Oh, Jesus, is this the one?"

After we had discussed the script, she said, "You don't remember me, do you?" Talk about getting off on the wrong foot! I had to admit that I couldn't place her. "My name is Gen Corick. I was a secretary at the Gospel Association about four years ago."

"Now I remember! You came as an answer to a prayer." And I told her the story about it. "Most of our volunteer secretaries, though they meant well, were incompetent. Then Steve Hart had hit on the solution. He reminded us, 'Christ said that according to your faith, it shall be done unto you. I believe we can apply that to our secretarial situation. If we have faith for a Model T secretary, that's what we'll get, so instead, let's all have faith for a Cadillac secretary.' Four days later, Gen, you joined us."

She flushed and laughed. "I never dreamed I was an answer to a prayer for a Cadillac." When she laughed, waves of joy flooded through me. All of a sudden I remembered something that stemmed the tide of excitement as quickly as it had started. The reason I hadn't tried to date her when she worked there before was because Bea had told me that she was spoken for. I stole a look at her hands folded in her lap. No rings!

As casually as I could, I asked, "Weren't you engaged then?"

"Not quite. We just went steady. But it didn't work out. And weren't you crazy over some girl named Jane?"

"Well, that never worked out either."

"I guess that gives us something in common then." Her laughter was as bright and promising as church bells on Easter morning. "How would you like to go on a boat ride up the Hudson tonight with our church group?" she asked. "The speaker is an old friend of yours from Zion Bible Institute in East Providence, Rhode Island, Reverend Leonard Heroo. He's often spoken of you, and I know he would like to see you again."

"I'd love to." Actually I would have loved to be anywhere she wanted me.

That night we leaned against the ship's railing and watched the moon rise over the Hudson. I was filled with a longing to know everything there was to know about her. Her voice was low and soft as she answered my questions.

"I was born in New York, of Russian parents. In fact, my mother was a White Russian." "That explains it," I exclaimed. "Nature has given you a sensitive, aristocratic outer beauty, and the Lord has given you a marvelous inner beauty, but there's also something else—a combination of old-world charm and feminine grace, all that was best about old Russia." I was laughing, but I meant it.

"I'm afraid I really don't have all those qualities," she smiled, "but my mother did. She really was beautiful."

"What was your father like?"

"Well, he was Russian too, but he came from a totally different background and could never really understand Mother. Besides, he drank heavily. It wasn't that he didn't love her. When he was sober, he could be very kind, but that became less and less frequent. She lived in fear of him, and finally her health broke and she died. I was nine at the time, and my brother Bill was seven. We were the youngest of six children. My older sisters tried to take over. They were wonderful to me but, of course, couldn't take the place of Mother. I missed her terribly."

"You had a sad childhood."

"Not really. There were many bright spots. One of the brightest was Marge Stankard. We've been friends since we were 12. From the very start we were like sisters and still are. What a gift of God she has been!"

"How did you come to know the Lord?"

"I believe that even as a child in the Presbyterian Church, I felt God's hand on my life. It was when I was 14 that I committed my life to the Lord at the Gospel Tabernacle in Astoria, New York. A year later I was baptized in the Holy Spirit."

The more Gen told me, the more I was drawn to her. With Jane, I had always felt I had to prove myself, but with this girl, I didn't feel I had to. I just wanted to protect her. I put my hand on her shoulder to comfort her and discovered that I yearned to wrap her in my arms, just from touching her. I urged her, "Go on. Tell me more."

"After high school, I went to work as a secretary. Then I worked in a bookstore, but the clerks would tell off-color stories, and it would embarrass me. I got another job, and then I sensed God's call to Bible school. I wanted very much to go but had no money. I prayed about it for weeks, and then one Sunday a graduate from Zion came to our church and told us what a wonderful school it was. When he said it was a faith school and charged no tuition fees, I, of course, was thrilled and knew this was God's provision. Zion was all I had hoped it would be and more. I had the experience that Jeremiah speaks of: 'Thy word was found and I did eat it and it was unto me the joy and rejoicing of my heart.' Those three years were the happiest years of my life.

"After that, Frances Cook, my roommate at Zion, and I pastored a church for two months in York, Pennsylvania, and I thought it was the beginning of my ministry. But then my father had a stroke, so I came back to the city to care for him. It was then that Bea Montanus asked me to come to the Gospel Association." She smiled. "That's when I met you, so I guess that's about all there is to my story."

But there was one thing more I had to know. And I didn't even want to ask it. I had known this girl for less than a day, and yet I found I could hardly bear it that she had been in love with someone else. "How long did you go steady?"

"It's hard to say. It was off and on. I thought I loved him, but I was afraid it wouldn't work out, that it wasn't part of God's plan."

"Do you still love him?" She didn't answer for a moment. A breeze blew up off the river, and she was standing so close by me I could feel the shiver that went through her body. Finally, in a low voice she answered, "No."

I hated for the evening to end. I had never felt like this before. The feelings I was experiencing were not the almost self-vindicating love I'd had for Jane, or the desire I felt for Leah. Certainly I couldn't have spent such an evening without feeling a strong attraction, but what I felt went on beyond the physical. Yet I hardly knew her, nor did I have any idea what she felt toward me.

When the boat docked, I walked back with her to her car. Until I had some assurance of how she felt, I didn't want her to guess the extent of my feelings for her. All I said was, "It's been a wonderful evening. I'd love to see you again."

She started the engine and waved good-bye with only a smile for an answer.

I called her the next day and saw her that night and the night after that. It was almost too good to be true. I couldn't believe that a girl as wonderful as Gen could actually be interested in me. After our third date, I came to work in the morning and found that she had left a little note on my desk:

Dear Harald,

Thank you for the last three nights. However, I do very much need a couple of evenings to take care of some personal matters. I know you'll understand. I've enjoyed your fellowship so much!

Sincerely, Gen

Fellowship! So that was what it was for her! My poor heart. One minute it seemed to be pounding out of me, and the next it would nearly stop. Here was the brush-off I had known was coming. All the rejection I had felt from Jane flooded in on me at that moment. Gen didn't want me either. Somehow, I went ahead with my work as if nothing was wrong, but inside, I was shredded.

At noon I was walking to the post office, unseeing, barely functioning. A car pulled up alongside of me. "Hi! Can I give you a lift?" It couldn't be! But it was. Gen.

"Sure." I got in, still torn up inside, and now completely bewildered. Had I misinterpreted her note? Had I typically, automatically, assumed the worst? Her sweetness was so natural, it couldn't be feigned. Oh, dear Jesus, nothing *had* changed! I believe that was the happiest moment of my life.

We dated so heavily for the next two weeks, and marriage was so much on my mind, that one night I panicked. I grew afraid that I was rushing into something that my years of bachelorhood had not prepared me for. I felt suddenly like I was trapped. That night Gen said, "You know, Harald, I think we are going pretty fast. I want you to know that you haven't committed yourself one little bit. Why don't you date other girls before we go any further?" The moment I knew I was free, I didn't want to be free. But wise Gen insisted that we both needed breathing space, and so it was agreed that we wouldn't see each other for a week. Since I knew it would be agony to be in New York and not be with her, I took that time to go to Florida and check on my parents.

Mother's eyesight was going, and Dad was losing his spryness. I wanted to find someone who would be able to come in daily and look after them. I interviewed a woman over the phone. She sounded lovely but was actually quite a surprise to look at. Agnes was middle-aged and quite cross-eyed. She was extremely thin, bowlegged and very tall; in fact, she was over six feet. But she took immediately to the folks, and they were delighted with her.

I told Mother and Dad very little about Gen, because I knew they would have a hundred questions I wasn't ready to answer. But while I was there, Norman called, and I told him, "I've met the most wonderful girl in the world. I'm sure she's the one." He was thrilled for me.

Back in New York, Gen and I took up where we'd left off. I'd known her exactly three weeks when I couldn't wait any longer. We sat in the car outside her house, and I begged, "Gen, I love you, body, soul, and spirit. I love you with all my heart. I love you so much I can't eat or think or sleep. Please marry me."

"I don't know, Harald; I can't tell you now. Everything's going so fast."

She started to kiss me lightly on the lips, but I held her fast and met her kiss with one that came from the depths of my soul. After that kiss, we sat in silence for a long time, and I basked in the joy of being so close to her. "That's all right, Gen. If you can't say yes tonight, I'll ask you tomorrow and the next day and the next, until you can."

I did. I begged her over and over again. One night we were driving on the New Jersey Turnpike when I asked for the hundredth time. "Gen, please marry me."

"All right, Harald, I will."

What irony! There was nothing I could do on that turnpike except keep on driving. I wasn't even concerned that her answer was almost cold; I just knew that she had agreed.

The next morning was Sunday, and when I went to get her for church, she threw her arms around me. "Harald, a wonderful thing has happened: Last night when I found myself saying yes to you, I was surprised at myself, because I was going to give you a noncommittal answer. But this morning when I told my brother Bill, 'I'm going to marry Harald,' I was overwhelmed with such a deep sense of peace and joy. I know now without a shadow of a doubt that marrying you is God's will for me."

For the next three weeks, we prepared for our marriage. I don't know if we ever did get all the invitations out. I'd say to her, "Let's just sit on the couch for a few minutes before we start addressing them." Once we sat down, we couldn't seem to get started on those invitations. Those last three weeks couldn't have seemed longer if they had been three years.

Sometime during that final waiting period, I answered the phone and found Norman at the other end. His voice was as distressed as could be. "Harald, please tell me you're not getting married."

"Of course I am."

"Look, couldn't we get together and talk it over first?"

"There's nothing to talk over. What's the matter with you anyway?"

"It's just that—well, I don't know how to say it..."

I couldn't figure him out. What I didn't know was that he had since been home and met Agnes, the woman who had gone to work for my folks, and Mother had introduced her as the girl Harald had found. He knew that I was getting married and had assumed that Agnes was the one. And so, as he persisted, I began to get a little annoyed. "Listen, Norman, before you say anything else, I think you'd better come on over to the Gospel Association at four o'clock, and you can meet her."

"No, not today. I'm ... tied up."

"Then get un-tied. Look, you're really going to love her."

There was a long pause. "Harald, I'll just put it on the line: These kinds of marriages never work out."

Now it was my turn to pause. "What do you mean?"

"I mean—" his voice sounded almost strangled "—that when one feels sorry for someone and marries them out of pity..."

"But, Norman, *I'm* the lucky one!"

"Oh, Harald..."

"Come on over, today. Four o'clock."

He muttered something that sounded like, "Might as well get it over with," and he hung up.

It was nearly five o'clock before he showed up, and when he arrived, it was obvious he'd been belting down a few. I'd no more than said, "Gen, this is

Norman," when he blurted, "*This* is the girl you're going to marry?"

"Yes."

He threw his arms around us both and burst into tears, then laughter, then tears again.

Dad and Mother were as eager to meet Gen as Norman had been reluctant. They arrived two days before the wedding, and I brought Gen home to Mama Looft's big old three-story house, where they were staying, to meet them. Dad met us at the door and looked at Gen with an expression of utter amazement. She hugged him and kissed his cheek. "Hello, Dad." He held her at arm's length, and his eyes clouded with tears. His voice shook, and he tried to cover his feelings with a joke. "Harald, I expected the barrel to have nothing but shriveled apples by the time you got there, and here you've brought home the pick of the crop."

Behind him, in her wheelchair, sat Mother. When she looked into Gen's face, she became radiant herself. "Oh, I just knew you'd look like this." Her eyes met mine. "She's a beautiful girl, son. A beautiful girl!" For once they were both happy with something I had done. Then I remembered who had done it, and I thanked Him.

Gen sat by the hour with Mother and said, "I wish you would tell me everything there is to know about Harald." How Mother loved to reminisce about long-ago days and her youngest son. And never once did she mention the disappointments I had brought her.

Seven weeks from the day Gen and I had met, we were married. Dad preached the wedding sermon and incorporated into it the choicest jewels from all the wedding sermons he had ever preached. Even though it went on a little longer than usual, everyone agreed it was a very moving service. In the receiving line, looking starry eyed, was Grace with her "recompense of reward." They had just returned from their honeymoon in time to attend our wedding. Since we couldn't afford a real reception, we served ice cream, cake and punch in the church hall.

Now as I look back on that time, I have to admit that though I loved Gen with all my heart, she was a far better wife to me than I was a husband to her. During our courtship, she had said, "As much as I have wanted to marry a man who was 100 percent sold on serving Jesus, I'm almost afraid to marry you, because you're the kind of man who would become so involved in ministering to someone, you'd forget all about me."

I had laughed at the mere suggestion, yet our honeymoon had scarcely begun before it happened. We were spending the night in a hotel en route to Florida, and I said to Gen, "I'll be right back. I'm just going down to the lobby for a paper."

"Oh fine. Would you get me a cup of coffee?"

I kissed her on the cheek and made a gallant bow. "Harald Bredesen at your service, madam."

I had every intention of getting the paper and coffee and coming right back, so I can't explain what happened. But when I got to the lobby, I somehow got into a conversation with the desk clerk and began witnessing to him about Jesus. An hour later I burst into our room.

"Gen, Gen! He's saved. He's accepted Jesus."

"Who's saved?"

"The desk clerk."

"Oh, I see. And where's my coffee?"

"I got so caught up talking to him I forgot all about it."

"I see you remembered your paper."

"Gen, I'm sorry. I'll go get it right away."

"Don't bother. The coffee shop is closed. I just called."

Nevertheless, our honeymoon was beautiful. It was a time of knowing and learning to know each other and growing in love. On our return to College Point, we found a cozy apartment that had an extra room for Gen's father. Gen used such imagination in decorating it and scouting out just the right used bargains to furnish it that coming home each night was always a new experience. She was able to fix marvelous meals on an impossible budget. Every day I'd see a new facet of her personality that kept me in a state of delighted amazement.

The first real difficulty we faced in our marriage occurred when Gen was six-months pregnant. We rushed to the hospital in the middle of the night, fully aware that something was wrong.

Several hours later, our baby was born, a son, weighing two pounds, nine ounces. I stood in front of the nursery window and watched him in his incubator. He was the tiniest human being I had ever seen, and I could hardly believe he was alive. Yet I could see his rib cage move up and down with every breath he took. He was my son, my firstborn, and I loved him. We named him Alfred after my father.

The doctor was honest. "Without oxygen he will die. With it, he will be blind and may still die." We told him to go ahead with the oxygen and kept on praying.

For 32 hours our son hung between life and death. Then his breathing grew more and more labored. The doctor came into Gen's hospital room at seven in the morning. "I'm sorry, Mrs. Bredesen..."

When I got to the hospital, Gen was crying. "Oh, Harald, I've never felt so empty-armed; I've never even held him, and yet I miss him so much."

Together we prayed, thanking Jesus. Even though we wept together, even though we felt a terrible sense of loss, our hearts were somehow peaceful. Jesus loved us—we both knew that—and He was our Comfort.

Before too long, Gen was expecting another baby, and our lives were filled with the promise of new life again. Our love for each other seemed to grow with every passing day.

I remember one night we were getting ready for bed and Gen began chuckling softly. "You know, I just thought of what my boss said when I told him I was going to marry you."

"What was that?"

"'You and Harald are older, and you're going to have a terrible time adjusting to marriage. My wife and I had quite a time, and we were young.' Oh, Harald—" she held her arms out to me and I wrapped mine around her "—it's been wonderful. Really. It hasn't been a hard adjustment at all."

# 15

There were the usual advertisements and the appeals in the morning mail that lay on my desk in the Gospel Association office. On the bottom of the pile was a square, off-white envelope that had the elegant look of something promising. I tore it open, and to my disappointment discovered it was only a ticket and invitation to the Christian Soldiers annual banquet. Back in the days of Cyril Mouland and Frank Birch, I had helped found the Christian Soldiers Mission, and every year following, I received a complimentary ticket to their dinner.

Every year I dropped it into the wastebasket, as Frank Birch had dropped me when I was in the hospital and needed him. But this year, almost without realizing it, I found myself reaching for a pen to acknowledge my acceptance. I was puzzled at my own actions. "Why am I breaking my pattern? Could this be God's inner direction? But why?"

The moment I entered the 23rd Street YMCA banquet room, I noticed a young man at the head table who was one of the speakers for the evening. He had such an open face and such a glow about him that I thought, *Now there is a man who knows the Lord Jesus.* The Lord spoke to me, *This is my reason for bringing you here tonight.*

The program stated his name, Pat Robertson. After the dinner I introduced myself to him. He was tall and lean with a mop of dark hair and an all-American football-hero smile. Later I often heard people comment on how closely he resembled John F. Kennedy—certainly they shared the same charisma, the same inborn qualities that make a man a leader of men.

He had been introduced as a Phi Beta Kappa student, a graduate of Yale Law School and the son of Virginia's distinguished senator, Willis A. Robertson, chairman of the Banking and Currency Committee. He had been a partner in an electronics-component firm when he had felt God's call to the ministry. Pat proudly introduced me to his attractive auburn-haired wife, Dede, who was as obviously in love with him as he was with her.

As we talked, I felt drawn to both of them. They were so easy to visit with, it was as if we had been friends for a long time. I was not at all surprised to find we were going to be taking the same subway home that evening. As we took our seats, I turned to Pat and asked, "Do you know anything about the Baptism in the Holy Spirit?"

"Funny you should ask. Just today in Washington, I met a fellow by the name of Bob Walker, the editor of *Christian Life* magazine, and he asked me the same question. He started to tell me about all the ups and downs of his life, and it was the perfect description of my own. But he said something tremendous had happened to him, and he was just going to tell me what this experience was when somebody interrupted."

"Bob Walker!" I marveled. "Well, I can complete that conversation, because Bob is a close friend. And I know his experience was the Baptism in the Holy Spirit." Pat was so fascinated and fascinating that it seemed our ride ended before we had hardly begun talking. A few days later I biked over to his house to bring him Stile's book, *The Gifts of the Spirit.*

He was dumbfounded. "You rode all the way over here?"

"Sure. I needed the exercise."

"That's fantastic. I can't get over it. You biked 10 miles just to bring me a book?" I learned that day that Pat had a way of making the ordinary seem spectacular. He gestured with his arms. "Come on in. Sit down. What can I get you?"

"Just a drink of water. I can't stay for long."

"You've got to stay long enough for me to tell you about the prayer group at the seminary. There's this group of all-out Christians who meet daily in the prayer tower to pray for a real outpouring of the Spirit."

"That's amazing. How did they get started?"

"First of all, we read about revival, and then we met a woman from Korea,

Su Nae Chu, who had experienced revival there. She showed us how everything begins with the Holy Spirit. Then someone got hold of the life story of Finney, the nineteenth-century evangelist who brought so many people to Christ. Anyway, we read about him and began to see that there was more to being a Christian than we realized. That's when we began praying for the Holy Spirit to empower us."

"Praise God! I'm quite a fan of Finney's." The spiritual power and effectiveness of the great lawyer-evangelist who shook America a hundred years ago had long fascinated me.

"You are? Great! You've got to meet these guys. We had quite an experience when we went on retreat. They'd love to tell you about it."

"I'd love to hear about it."

"How about tomorrow night? Would you come to our prayer meeting?"

"Sure."

We talked on and on, and it was after dark when I biked back to our apartment. Pat Robertson had become a friend on the night of the banquet, but this afternoon, as we shared our hopes and our dreams, he became a true brother in Jesus Christ. As I pedaled up to our doorway, I called out, "Thank You, Jesus, for sending me to the Christian Soldiers banquet."

I went to the meeting the next night, never dreaming what a lasting effect it would have on my life. Pat and Dede were there. With them were another very attractive couple, Dick Simmons and his wife, Barbara, and other live-wire seminarians, among them Dick White, Lois Ostensen, Alice Blair, and the student body president, Gene Peterson.

I heard the amazing story of how these young people, while on retreat and reading about Finney, discovered an old sign that told them the very farmhouse in which they were staying was his birthplace. They were so eager to receive all that the Spirit had to give that I found myself loving each one of them. I then shared my own experience, and we prayed and praised God.

In time, everyone in that group received the Baptism in the Holy Spirit.

Later we were joined by Paul Morris, the pastor of Hillside Avenue Presbyterian Church, and eventually we began meeting in his church regularly. It became a time of marvelous fellowship, one of mutual love and encouragement, as these young people became my spiritual family.

No sooner had these new friendships been formed than a trio of events occurred that were the beginning of a whole new direction in my life. One morning I came to work and found a letter on my desk from Dr. Schiotz, the president of the American Lutheran Church. He wanted to know if I was ready to settle down and take a parish. This was a surprise, because during the trouble at Pine Bluff, I had resigned from the Lutheran ministry. Later I found out that they had never acted on my resignation, because by one of God's coincidences, Joe Belgum (good old Joe!) happened to be at headquarters when my resignation arrived. He said, "History has proved that whenever the Lutheran church has severed ties with one of its sons, it has lived to regret the day."

But since I thought I had resigned, the letter was quite unexpected. I answered:

Dear Dr. Schiotz:

Thank you very much for writing me about a parish. However I do not feel called to be a pastor, nor do I have any plans to leave my present position...

Shortly after that, I was praying with Dick and Pat and the rest of our group when I felt the hand of God upon me. There, as I was praising God with my friends, the glory of God came down upon me so strong that I couldn't kneel. I leaped to my feet while a torrent of words in a tongue I had never heard before poured out of the depths of my being. I was overwhelmed with a sense of the marvelousness of God's love and His grace. I wanted to proclaim the gospel everywhere. I had always dreaded going into the ministry because of having to preach; now I longed for the chance to tell everyone about Jesus.

Later, going home, I said to Pat, "I wonder what this means? Could God be calling me to preach?"

It was the very next day that the phone on my desk rang. "Harald? Come over here right away. Something's happened!" It was Mama Looft.

I dashed to her house. "Mama, what is it?"

"I've had a vision."

"A vision?"

"Yes, of you. I saw you preaching in this church. There was a baptismal font on your left as you stood in the pulpit and on your right was a pipe organ. Gen was in front of it, and the women of the church were clustered around her. They seemed so delighted to have her for their new minister's wife!"

"Where was this church?"

"I don't know, but I saw the grounds around the church, and they were quite extensive. To the back and to the left, there was a parsonage."

This was a pretty detailed description, and I knew there was no such church around. It was this one fact that made Mama's vision convincing; she loved Gen and me too much to wish us out of town.

I left her house, wondering what it could all mean, wondering how it tied in with last night's experience of wanting to preach, knowing that something was about to happen.

As the day wore on, I realized deep within me that a longing *had* been there ever since those pre-ordination days when Joe and I had first talked about a call. Somewhere in the depths of my soul, I knew I really did want to be a pastor.

Two mornings later, a caller identified herself on the phone as Mabel Nelson, president of the United Council of Church Women in the Bronx. "Reverend Bredesen, would the fact that you are a Lutheran minister keep you from accepting a call to a Reformed church? We are the Dutch equivalent of the Scotch Presbyterian."

She went on to explain: "You see, there is this church in Mount Vernon, just north of New York in Westchester County. It has been without a pastor for three years."

Westchester County ... what scenes of wealth and beauty those words recalled—stately mansions on majestic bluffs overlooking the broad blue Hudson, scenic riding trails by rushing brooks, vast expanses of woodsy greenness in close proximity to New York. All these had made the county a favorite residential area for those who could afford it, among them Dr. Knapp whom I used to visit in Mount Vernon when I worked for him. Westchester was now the wealthiest county in the world. "Tell me," I asked, "what is the church like?"

"It's of Tuckahoe marble, a jewel of architecture—a bit of old England put down in a park-like setting, a block deep in the heart of Mount Vernon. It's famous for its stained-glass windows, the most beautiful in the county. They were executed in Germany about a hundred years ago when the church was built. There are 12 windows depicting the life of Christ, and a rare rose window that is out of this world."

"Does it have a pipe organ?"

"Oh, yes. A large one, but I've never heard it."

The moment Mrs. Nelson hung up, I phoned Gen. "I just had a call to be a pastor!"

"Oh, Harald, that's wonderful! Where and who and when?"

I told her all I knew. "It's only a half hour from here. Come on, let's go and see it during lunch."

"I can't. Papa isn't feeling at all well. I don't think I should leave him. But Mama Looft and Hal Miller I know would love to go."

Hal, our old friend, was up visiting us from Florida. He was so much fun and so helpful that we always made him prolong his stays. He hopped into my old Studebaker, and we dropped by to pick up Mama Looft. She was right in the middle of a wash, but wiped her hands and dropped everything to go with us. We took the scenic Hutchinson River Parkway and watched for the first Mount Vernon exit.

As we left the lovely parkway and drew near the church, the scenery began changing drastically. I could not believe my eyes. The houses were old, many of them run-down. The streets were garbage-strewn, and two blocks from the church was a low-cost housing project, a ghetto surrounded by worn-out houses, grocery stores and taverns.

I pulled up at the curb and asked a policeman, "Is this really Mount Vernon?"

"Sure. What's your problem?"

"I used to come here 15 years ago. I just can't believe that this is the same city I remember."

"A lot of things can happen to a town in 15 years, especially this one. It has the fastest population shift of any suburb in this and the surrounding four states. And nearly all of it here on the south side. The north side is still pretty much the Mount Vernon you probably remember."

We pulled away from the curb and drove the two remaining blocks to the church. There it was, in all its ancient beauty, oblivious to its surroundings, perfectly preserved, looking as if it had been standing for centuries. Mama Looft was the first one out of the car, and in spite of her three score and ten years, she went up the stone steps and through the gate of the church so fast that we had to hustle to keep up with her. "See there?" she puffed, pointing with her cane. "There's the parsonage in the back to the left, just as I saw it!"

We stepped into the church and suddenly a pall came over me. If the exterior had seemed in perfect condition, the inside of the church looked as if it had not had any work done since its erection. The lofty ceilings were all sooty and gray, and in some places the plaster was actually beginning to fall. The carpeting on the floor was so old and faded it would have been impossible to describe its color. The lead in the gorgeous stained-glass windows was corroding. No wonder there hadn't been a pastor in three years! There probably weren't more than 200 members left.

I heard a soft sigh beside me. It was Hal, looking around and shaking his head. "Harald, this is not the place for you. God has something much better for you than this."

But Mama Looft was exuberant. "See? There is the baptismal font just as I saw it and the pulpit where you were preaching. And over here is the organ console where Gen was standing, surrounded by the ladies of the church. Everything is just exactly as I saw it."

I was grateful for the confirmation of her vision, but I didn't need it. I knew in my heart that this was the church to which God was calling me. I could hardly wait to get back and tell Gen.

That night we sat on the Hide-a-bed and talked for hours. Gen's eyes were shining. "Harald, it will be a new life for you."

I reached for her hand and held it in mine. "It will be a new life for both of us. For all three of us."

"I know. It will be wonderful to have the baby grow up in a small town. Ever since Dagni was born a year ago, I've wanted her growingup years to be special. I know they will be, there."

"And you'll be beautiful as the pastor's wife."

"And, Harald, think of your father. He'll be so proud that you finally have a church."

"Yes, but let's not count our chickens. We haven't been accepted yet."

"But we will be. I know it in my heart that we will." But how, I wondered, would this church receive my witness to the Baptism and gifts of the Holy Spirit.

The night before I went to be interviewed, I prayed for a long time. "Jesus, shall I tell them I speak in tongues?" The answer seemed to come, *Answer them forthrightly but volunteer nothing.*

My next letter home glowed with the old enthusiasm, but this time it was different; I wasn't kidding myself.

Dear Mother and Dad,

I have been called to historic First Reformed Church of Mount Vernon, New York. It's a church you both would love because it would bring to mind the churches and parsonages of Norman's and my early days. I hope the fact that this is not a Lutheran church won't spoil it for you, and that you will be as happy as I am.

Dad replied:

Dear Harald,

Even if you are not in the Lutheran church, at least your

ministry is in a historic church. We are grateful that at last you have a pastorate. Please don't do anything foolish and jeopardize this chance. You have made us both very happy and proud.

I couldn't speak when I read that. It felt so good to know that at last they were proud of me. They weren't the only ones who were pleased. At First Reformed, George and Anna Wedlake, a brother and sister who, like their parents before them, wielded tremendous influence in the life of the church, were delighted we had come. Neither had married, and they had made the church their life and the congregation their family. We were to meet them at the church the day after I had been accepted by the board, to discuss our living arrangements.

We arrived before they did, and it gave Gen and me a moment to take in the surroundings of our new home. It was late summer, and the magnificent trees around the church framed it like a beautiful picture. In my arms, I held our little blonde, blue-eyed Dagni and watched as her eyes discovered a pigeon that had come to rest on the top of the church's varicolored slate roof. Beside me I heard Gen catch her breath. "It *is* beautiful here. God is so good."

If only I had been half as generous with her that afternoon as God had been with me, the pattern of our tenure at this new church may have taken on a different design. But 36 years of bachelorhood had not prepared me for the down-to-earth unselfishness that marriage requires.

For the moment the sky was cloudless, and we basked in the sunshine of promise. A taxi stopped, and the Wedlakes stepped out. "Pastor Bredesen, Mrs. Bredesen." Their outstretched hands and beaming smiles made us feel how genuinely glad they were to have us. "Come and let us show you the apartment we picked out for you and your family."

All of a sudden I felt a shadow cross the perfectness of the day. "An apartment? Aren't we going to live in the manse?"

Anna gasped. "Oh no, Pastor. It's too big and inconvenient, and it's in terrible disrepair. We haven't used it as a parsonage for years."

But in my mind I already pictured us living there. "Can't we look at it? From the outside it doesn't look bad at all, and I can see it has been freshly painted."

There was silence, and then George shrugged and led the way to the back of the church. "I guess there's no harm in looking if you really want to."

As we stepped into the kitchen, a mouse darted across the warped floor and hid in the woodwork. Behind us, the old wooden door rusting on its hinges creaked shut. "Brrr," Gen said, shivering beside me. "That sounded like the opening of a radio mystery thriller."

Yet despite the musty smell, the faded wallpaper, and the tall narrow windows, there was a graciousness about the old house that I loved. One by one we went through the manse's 11 rooms. In every one the walls were grey, sooty and irregular, and the ceilings were crisscrossed with cracks, as if it were about to fall. But I could imagine the laughter that had echoed there in days gone by, when the rooms had been filled to overflowing with children and relatives and guests.

Our tour ended up back in the kitchen. It was enormous, and Gen groaned when she really looked at it. "Look: one, two, three, four, four, five, six, seven doors."

"That's a good scriptural number," I said. "Just look at that old brick fireplace right in the kitchen. How cozy!"

"Yes, and there's not a place for a cupboard or proper work space. What an incredible relic." She and Anna Wedlake burst out laughing. "Can you just imagine fixing dinner for a family, not to mention company?"

For some reason I hated them making fun of the old house.

# 16

"Gen, you know this place reminds me of the boyhood parsonages I grew up in?"

She had found one of the two pantries and answered from there. "It's probably been that long since anything was modernized and repaired."

"But just think what it would be like if it were fixed up," I countered as she came back into the room. Then, avoiding her eyes, I turned to George who was still picking cobwebs off his coat from our excursion into the attic. "Would the church budget swing the repairs?"

"I very much doubt it."

"Well, it doesn't matter," Gen said. "We couldn't possibly live here. Come on, Harald, let's go and see the apartment they have picked out for us."

"But, Gen, I want to live here."

She looked at me as if she couldn't believe I was serious. "Harald, how could I possibly look after this place and take care of Dagni and Papa and help you with your ministry?"

I was hurt and disappointed that she didn't share my vision of the place, and without thinking, I answered, "My mother was able to do it."

In the following silence, the words stood cold and hard between us. I knew I had been wrong, but I rationalized, "Doesn't the Bible say that a man should be head of his wife? Shouldn't his wife be submissive?"

Gen said no more. When the church agreed to pay for the materials if I would find the volunteer labor to fix it up, I decided that we would live in the manse. It was a grossly selfish decision and if I had thought further of Paul's exhortation, I would have realized that he was talking about love, not bullheaded domination. Because of my stubbornness that day, the first bitter seeds of resentment toward me were planted in Gen's heart.

The first few months with the church started like our marriage, with a wonderful honeymoon. Everyone in the congregation, it seemed, was overjoyed and welcomed us with open arms. The women came daily to the manse and helped to get it in order. Everyone who came fell in love with Gen, and she loved them all. In fact, Gen seemed so happy that I forgot how much she wanted the house—especially the kitchen—fixed. The volunteer labor I had promised to find was hard to come by, and the new sink the church had provided sat uninstalled on the floor beside the radiator.

Some mornings I would wake up and just marvel at the joy of being a pastor. From the beginning, I preached evangelical sermons, but the congregation didn't mind. "After all," I once heard George say, "those Billy Graham sermons are going to bring in people from the outside, and this is what this church needs."

We'd been there just a year, when Dad came for a visit. Mother was in a nursing home by now, but knowing how much he wanted to see my new church, she had urged him to come. As soon as he stepped off the train, he began shivering in his light Florida suit that was scant protection against the cool northern air. "It's cold country you've chosen, son."

I laughed. "Here, Dad, you'd better wear my coat." As I put it around his shoulders, a shiver went through me. Not because of the cold, but because I feared we were off on the wrong track with Dad complaining about the weather. I realized then just how much I wanted Dad to approve of my new pastorate.

Gen greeted him at the doorway of the manse with a hug and a kiss. And he hugged her back. "You're still as beautiful as ever, I see. I hope this son of mine has been taking good care of you."

"He has, Dad."

"Good. Now first things first. Where's my Dagni?"

"Here I am, Gampa."

He scooped her into his arms and sat down with her on the davenport. "She's the image of you, Harald," he exclaimed. "Why this little thing here is so much like you that I could be back in Bricelyn with you on my knee." He hugged her and kissed her and held her until she wiggled free. He took off his glasses and rubbed his eyes. "I remember how I used to bounce you on my knee and tell Mother how someday you'd succeed me in the ministry." Then, finding Dagni and holding her hand, he walked around the manse. "Beautiful, beautiful," he murmured. "Your mother would love this place." In the kitchen he stopped before the old brick fireplace. "Do you remember the old black stove we used to have, and how your mother would stand there toward suppertime stirring fløte grøt?"

"I remember." Actually I remembered very well. She had been making cream gruel when Dad and I had the argument and I insisted I would never go into the ministry.

At length, I asked, "Dad, would you like to see my church?"

"I certainly would. Now where did Gen put that coat of yours?"

Inside the church, he seemed to see none of the disrepair. "Just look at those tremendous crossbeams and those magnificent walnut pews. There isn't a church anywhere that could afford them today. And that rose window! It's exquisite! And those side windows! They are the most beautiful I have ever seen anywhere."

"Even in the Lutheran church, Dad?"

"Even in the Lutheran church, son."

"Dad," I suddenly asked, "would you like to preach at the Sunday service?"

"Harald, it would be an honor."

When Sunday came, he stood in the pulpit, looking as if he belonged there. He seemed to know just how to preach to the people. Instinctively, he warmed their hearts by commenting on the windows and architecture. His sermon was one of his best, Christcentered and laced with pathos and humor. He had us all laughing one moment and crying the next.

I was so proud. I felt a melting love for him and could sense his love for me. "Thank You, Jesus," I whispered. I struggled to keep back the tears but finally gave up and wept unashamedly.

After the service, he stood under the balcony in the social area of the church and visited with my parishioners. He seemed to have a droll story to fit every occasion, and I could tell by their comments that the people adored him. George Wedlake said to me, "We have great hopes for you, Harald, if you turn out just like your father."

Dad preached again the following Sunday, and then left, eager, I know, to get back and share with Mother his visit to their son's church. I didn't know how much it had all meant to him, however, until a letter came a short time later, just two years before he died.

Dear Harald,

I believe that the proudest moment of my life came last week when I stood in your pulpit and spoke in your church. Maybe I'm just an old man reminiscing, but it was something I've dreamed of doing ever since you were a boy, something I never lost hope for. I could tell that your congregation accepted me, and I felt I was a help in getting you started, something else I admit I always thought I would do.

God bless you, son, and Gen and our little Dagni. Mother and I pray for you all daily and for your church.

# 17

The honeymoon with the church that Dad had witnessed lasted for a year. During that time I gave up my Lutheran affiliation and was installed as the pastor. After that I expected things to go even better, that the small congregation would grow, that they would become more and more my flock and I their shepherd.

Yet that wasn't the way it went. It seemed to me that no one was as pleased with me as they had once been. Not nearly so often did I see those looks of approval on their faces or hear the words of encouragement that had meant so much during that first year. But the complaints increased, little ones mostly, and I felt a growing spirit of dissatisfaction in the air.

One day when I was feeling particularly down, the most erudite woman in the church said, "You know, you are really not our kind of pastor. My husband and I wanted someone who is intellectual, but for the sake of the others, we went along with their choice."

Someone else said, "Last Sunday, you officiated at the worst Communion service I have ever seen. You walked in front of the Communion table instead of in back. It seemed so disrespectful." From then on, I was anxious over every worship service, wondering if I would do something else wrong.

A consistory man said, "Pastor, I don't approve of your friends. I saw one of them throw his Bible irreverently on the pew." I cautioned my young prayer partners from biblical seminary to be more careful, but after that I was always a little nervous when too many of them were around.

As each day went by, I felt with mounting dread that as pastor, and therefore as a person, I was falling short. I woke up one morning and pushed my legs over the edge of the bed. Across my back the muscles ached like the first day of haying season back on the farm. The heavy weight of failure pulled at my shoulders as I stood up.

"Oh, Gen, what's gone wrong? There are so many people here who don't like me that I don't know which way to turn."

She tried to comfort me. "Just do your best, that's all God asks. Besides, I believe you are much better liked than you realize."

That wasn't enough. I still longed to be a really effective and successful pastor.

I invited Pat Robertson to be my student pastor. As Pat was one of the finest, most anointed Bible teachers I had ever met, I was confident he would win over the people. However, as great as it was to be working with him, something devastating occurred that I hadn't counted on. Being around him created for me a far worse tension than even the criticisms of the parishioners. His stature and good looks made me feel like once again I was walking in Norman's tall, handsome shadow. One day I looked in on his Bible class, and he was so inspired and the people so attentive, my heart sank as I realized how little my own Bible studies offered in comparison. As we worked side by side, I was aware of my own lack in a way that I had never been aware of it before.

Pat's youthful confidence in what he believed was so contagious that sometimes I found myself going along with it in spite of inner misgivings. For example, though we both believed that the arrangement of the chancel, the front of the church, was all wrong, I probably wouldn't have done anything about it if Pat hadn't felt so strongly. Originally the huge walnut pulpit that now stood on the side had been in the middle, but a beloved pastor who put on dramatizations rather than sermons had moved it to the side. When the pastor left, an altar with a brass cross and two candlesticks had been put in the middle.

Pat and I had been pacing up and down praying in the church when Pat paused and said, "You know, we ought to put that pulpit right smack back in the center of the church where John Calvin said it should be, where the founders of this church designed it to be, and where it symbolizes the centrality of the proclamation of the Word."

"Pat, I think you're right. It does belong in the middle. But what will the consistory say? Or the people of the church?"

"The first thing we've got to decide, Harald, is what is right. And we both agree this is right."

I could not but agree.

That evening Gen was standing at the ironing board in the dining room when I said, "Pat and I are going to move the pulpit back to the center of the church where it belongs."

Gen stopped ironing and stood with the iron in mid-air. "You're going to do what?"

"Move the pulpit back to the center and the altar to the side."

"Oh, Harald, you're not. The people *chose* to put the altar there. It is a gift from the Chinese Sunday school and means so much to them."

"Do you know what someone in my prayer group said about that altar? That it looks as if it is about to cave in under the weight of all the memorial gifts it has to carry. We also feel that the people here are only playing church with their candles and shiny brass altar ware. And speaking of candles—"

"And speaking of your prayer group," Gen burst in, "they are not even members of this church, and you are listening to them as if they were the voice of God. I wish you would listen to me for once. Believe it or not, I can actually hear from God, too. But you would never admit that."

"Of course I would, but I also know that Saint Paul says a husband is tempted to please his wife instead of pleasing God, and I'm leaning over backward not to do that."

"You are indeed. But, Harald, don't lean so far you break your back, your church, and our marriage. It could happen, you know."

Gen silently resumed her ironing.

On the night the consistory met, Pat and I had already moved the altar to the back far corner of the choir stall and pushed the old heavy walnut pulpit to the center. George Wedlake was out of town for the meeting, and after we explained to those present why we had moved it, they unanimously approved of our idea. When George returned, he was aghast, as was the entire Sunday school faculty and many others. Finally, after much dissension, hard feelings and anger, the matter was put up to a vote.

We won, but Gen called it a hollow victory. She shook her head. "What a terrible price you have paid to have your own way. You have permitted an issue of no spiritual importance to split the church. Now, when you say there are people in this church who don't like you, I'll have to agree; in fact, they'll have my sympathy."

Incredibly, it didn't occur to me at the time that my wife's will and God's will could be one and the same; in fact, that in this instance He might be trying to speak to me through Gen.

The incident with the chancel furniture established a pattern for my actions. I was started on a path from which there was no turning back, where the voice of my friends drowned out that voice within that so often agreed with Gen.

Whatever the ills of the church, Pat and I were agreed on the solution. What we needed was revival, just like the ones Finney had had 125 years ago.

It was reported that Finney was so full of God that all he had to do was look a sinner in the eye and the man would burst into tears. "Bringing sinners to repentance," Finney said, "is a process of burning down all the underbrush behind which they hide, smoking them out of their subterfuges, until at length they stand naked before God." His favorite Scripture verse was Jeremiah 23:29: "Is not my word like as a fire?... and like a hammer that breaketh the rock in pieces?"

Week after week, I preached the gospel according to Finney. Never did a Sunday go by that I didn't have my congregation over the fire or under the hammer. The only problem was, they didn't melt and they didn't crumble. They got harder. And the harder they got, the harder I got.

I remember the morning I stepped into my pulpit knowing I had a sermon that would not fail to convict them and trigger the revival for which I longed. Finney, I was sure, would have been proud of me. And I could see from Pat's expression that he certainly was. I started my sermon by shouting,

"Repent." I repeated the word again louder, "Repent!" And then, with still greater emphasis, I repeated it the third time. *"Repent!"* The congregation fidgeted nervously in their seats, but I pulled out my hammer and went to work. I started on the Sunday school faculty. "You teachers, don't think you are saved just because you recited the Creed the day you joined the church or because you teach a class. Until you admit that you are lost, hell-bound sinners and repent and turn to Jesus, you are still in your sins. You are still as lost as any Bowery derelict. In fact, you are even worse off than a derelict, because at least he knows he's lost."

Next to come under my hammer were the elders. And before my sermon was over, there was not a member or officer of that church whom I had missed. One by one the faces of the people began to reflect their outraged feelings. George and Anna Wedlake stared in openmouthed disbelief. A fuel-oil contractor, one of the biggest contributors, grew red-faced with anger. Several women began talking among themselves and shaking their heads. A young lady crossed her arms in a gesture of hostility, and her eyes flashed resentment. Gen kept looking at the floor, her face a flush of embarrassment.

Afterward, George came to me as a spokesman for the church. "Pastor," he said gently, "we don't feel it's right for you to preach these wild tent-meeting sermons every Sunday." He pleaded with me. "Please, would you not do it for a while?"

"Look here, George, I have to preach like this if anything is going to happen. We have elders on our consistory who are not saved, and it says right in the constitution that to function in the role of elders, they must have experienced salvation. Not only am I going to keep on preaching, but I'm going to personally examine every Sunday school teacher and consistory man and find out for myself if they are saved."

"But, Pastor, the teachers and elders *are* saved."

"And if I find out they are not, there'll be some changes!"

George shook his head and left. I was sure he'd go home and tell his sister that they had made a mistake, that the new pastor was impossible. But his words only made me more determined.

The next Sunday, Pat, too, picked up the hammer and told the congregation, "*Agape* love is the love of the unlovable, and that's the kind of love I have for you. There is nothing lovable about any of you. None of you are good, or personable, or handsome, or attractive in any way. I couldn't love a one of you if God didn't give me a supernatural love for you..."

The people of First Reformed Church again blinked their eyes in amazement. Never had they been told that they were unlovable. Gen, too, disapproved. That night she sat on the edge of the bed and brushed her hair for so long, I knew she was working up the courage to say something. Finally she blurted, "Harald, I think you and Pat are far too harsh. Many of these people already *have* a relationship with Jesus, and the ones who don't will have to see more of His love in you before they'll want Him."

But Pat was young and full of zeal, and I was 37 and full of insecurity. It was a difficult combination to reckon with.

True to my word to George, Pat and I took on the Sunday school faculty and began to examine them and to see if they were born again. One night at an informal meeting, one bright young fellow by the name of Henry Stormenger, Jr., who was the son of the clerk of the consistory, said, "Well, I went to the Billy Graham meeting last night. That should count for something."

"Did you go forward?"

"No."

I don't know why I kept saying things that made a bad situation worse, but I asked, "Was it because you weren't good enough, or because you were too good?"

While he sputtered at my judgmental question, the rest of the faculty grew obviously furious.

Afterward, when I related to Gen what I had told Henry, she was almost as upset as he had been.

Later that evening she handed me the Ann Landers newspaper column. "Here, read this."

It was a letter from a psychologist about a girl who, after jilting one suitor after another, ended up unmarried. He explained that it was her subconscious fear of their rejecting her that caused her to "beat them to the draw."

"Well, what's the point you're making, Gen?"

"The point is, Harald, that this is exactly what you are doing to your congregation. It's your fear of their rejecting you that's making you reject them."

"But I don't reject them!"

"No, not in so many words, but in the very way you talk and preach to them; you give them the Word like the jab of a spear. Subconsciously you are saying to yourself, 'When they reject me, it won't be because I have failed but because I have fearlessly proclaimed Jesus and they have rejected Him.'"

"Gen, please stop trying to psychoanalyze me. If I'm being hard on these people it's only because I want to bring them to a sense of their need.

Finney says that to offer the gospel to a man before you have brought him to a sense of his need is like offering water to a man who isn't thirsty."

"Please, Harald, *stop* trying to be Finney! Stop trying to be Pat Robertson. Be Harald Bredesen, the warm, loving man I married."

I thought it would help if the Sunday school faculty heard the same message of salvation from another speaker, so I invited them all to a friend's house for a meeting and then tipped off the speaker that they needed to be saved.

I knew by their faces as the speaker focused completely on them that they were indignant. One man grew so red that I thought he would explode. I had talked to him the week before, and I knew he was relying on his church membership for his salvation and not Jesus, but I just couldn't seem to approach him or any of the people in the church gently, as I had the people I hitched rides with in Florida. My only method was to ram salvation down their throats, hoping that if I rammed it far enough it would reach their hearts.

One night I was called to the bedside of a man who had had a heart attack. I said to him, "If you were to pass on, what would you rely on for salvation?"

"That I've always been a good man."

Because he was so close to death, I had to explain to him that Jesus was his only hope. After I left, he had a terrible heart attack. So it got to be that, frequently, when someone was in the hospital, the pastor wasn't notified for fear he would come and talk with him.

Pat and I decided to visit every home in the parish. In the home of one of our deacons, the contractor who had gotten so angry with my salvation sermon, we found him in the attic pounding on a new partition for his house. "I'm sorry, Pastor. I can't take time to talk to you. But if you want to talk while I hammer, go ahead." While he pounded, I talked about his need of a Savior, until he finally laid his hammer down, folded his hands across his chest, and said, "Pastor, I'm going to be frank with you; whenever you stand up in that pulpit and open your mouth, I reach for a little knob inside of me and turn you off so that I don't hear a word until you stop preaching."

From then on, I hated going into the pulpit. Every Sunday as I looked across the congregation, all I could see were little knobs switching off one by one.

I knew that it was only a matter of time before the whole church body disintegrated. What could I do? Bringing Pat hadn't helped. Finney-like tactics were useless. My messages fell on deaf ears.

On sleepless nights, so as not to disturb Gen, who was expecting our second baby, I would get out of bed and go into the cold, dark church to pace back and forth in the silence calling out, "Jesus, what am I doing wrong? Help me..."

But something was blocking our communications. For the first time in my life I couldn't seem to hear Him.

# 18

And now I come to the chapter of my life that is the most painful of all to share. How anyone could be as blind and insensitive to the one whom God had given him and whom he dearly loved is as difficult for me to relate as it may be for the reader to understand. But if this book is to be honest, I must tell it.

The problem between us actually began that day I decided that we would live in the manse, completely disregarding Gen's objections. Once we moved in, I couldn't resist bringing people home to fill those empty rooms.

For too many years before my marriage, I had stood with my face pressed against the window of other people's happiness. Now that I was experiencing such happiness of my own, I ached for everyone I met who still stood on the outside looking in.

There was Bob, who was paranoid and who couldn't keep a job; Tony, who was just a youngster down on his luck; John, who had run away from his fifth foster home when I found him crying in the back of the church; and Maria, who was on parole for forgery. There was Al, who had been asked to leave the seminary after he had received the Baptism. There were Carole and Mike and Esther and many more that I can't even remember now.

For all of them I had great empathy and was thrilled each time the Lord touched one of their lives. Since our three-story manse had so many rooms, it seemed almost a sin against charity not to invite them home. Though these extra people were making more work for Gen, I persuaded myself that eventually they would become a help to her, and meanwhile, since this was the life to which God was calling us, He would give her the extra strength and grace she needed. I prayed that she would learn to appropriate them.

There were so many in and out that once, several years later at a convention, a man spoke to Gen and seemed quite surprised she didn't remember him. "Why, Mrs. Bredesen, I stayed in your home for almost a week." She apologized, "I'm sorry, there were just too many people to remember." She told me one night, "I've been keeping track, Harald, and this past year we have had an average of 11 people sitting down to dinner every evening."

Gradually the welcome she extended became tolerance, and then tolerance turned to frustration. I first became aware of her feelings, although she said she had tried to talk to me about them before, one night when I brought Pat Robertson home for dinner. Gen was in the kitchen stirring something on the stove. Meg, our second little daughter, was fussing, and Maria was rocking her back and forth saying, "I can't get her to quit crying, Mrs. Bredesen." Dagni was holding onto Gen's leg with every step she took. The racket from the front room where the boys were scuffling could be heard even in the kitchen.

I should have sized up the situation, used my head, and waited before springing my question, or even had enough sense not to spring it at all. Instead, I stood in the middle of the floor to get Gen's attention. "Honey, I met a young convict today who is trying to go straight, and he has had the most heartbreaking— " BAM! She slammed the pan down on the stove and wheeled around. Sparks almost shot from her eyes.

"No! Absolutely not!"

"No, what?"

"No, he's not coming here. Every room—even the attic—is full." There was a butcher-knife sharpness to her voice. "But there's still room in the basement."

"No, Harald, no, no, *no!*" Her voice rose with every no until she was almost yelling. "Please don't ask another thing of me."

I was dumbfounded. She had never raised her voice like that before.

Pat and Maria stared at her, openmouthed. The noise from the front room stopped in an instant. Meg's crying and Dagni's whimpering were the only noises in the room.

Gen snapped at me. "Would you take that baby and do something with her?" Then she snapped at Pat, too. "Would you pick up Dagni and take care of her until dinner? That would be doing something useful for a change."

Pat picked her up and backed hastily out of the kitchen. Maria handed me Meg, and I backed out too. I heard a cupboard door slam and saw a somber-appearing Maria walked into the dining room with her arm full of plates. From the look she gave me, I couldn't tell what she was thinking.

Pat and I took the girls out on the porch, and he began to make excuses for not staying for dinner. I was humiliated enough as it was, without him walking out on me. "No, Pat, stay. I need all the help I can get."

That night taught me a lesson, but not the one I really needed to learn. From then on, whenever I felt someone needed a place to stay, I brought them home without asking Gen first. I trusted her compassion enough to know that when she met them and heard their story, she wouldn't turn them away.

Another problem between us was Sunday dinner. It was my thinking that Gen should realize how much I needed her support in the church and that she should at least honor my wishes about inviting company home for a meal after the Sunday service. I knew of other pastors who always invited people home every week. Over the years I had been a Sunday guest in many parsonages.

One Sunday a man from Chicago brought a group of 28 people from New York to our morning service. I invited them all to dinner. "Go on back to the parsonage. Just walk in. My wife will be delighted."

By the time I got there, young people were all over the front steps and yard. Everyone seemed in an unusually good mood, and an hour passed in no time. After that, I began to think it strange Gen hadn't called us for dinner. I excused myself and went into the house and back into the kitchen. There were several women there, but no Gen. "Do you know where my wife is?"

"No, we thought she was held up talking to someone."

"Oh well, maybe she's upstairs." I dashed upstairs and checked each room, but again no Gen. Somehow, with the help of the girls who stayed with us, dinner got served without her, and the guests finally left.

I hadn't been worried at first, just perplexed, but as the afternoon wore on, and Gen didn't appear, I began to grow apprehensive. Where had she gone? What had happened to her? I asked one of the girls on our staff, Barbara Judd, a student at Nyack Missionary Training School, to stay with Dagni and Meg, and I began a search of the neighborhood and the church.

"Gen? Gen?" I poked my head in each Sunday school class in the Christian education building, my voice resounding strangely in every silent room. In the church I called her name, and the walls echoed back. Still there was no answer. I checked the office, each cubicle, even the grounds.

I cornered the custodian. "Do you know where Gen is?"

He shook his head. "Why, no, I don't, but why not ask Mr. Wedlake? He seems to know just about everything goin' on in this church."

"No, that's all right, thank you." George and Anna Wedlake were the last people I wanted to have know that the pastor wasn't able to locate his wife on Sunday afternoon. By five o'clock my only emotion was fear. Where could she be? Was she dead somewhere? No, no, she couldn't be. But where *was* she? I went back to the manse and checked every room again.

At five-thirty Gen walked in the front door.

"You're home. Are you all right?"

"I'm fine," she said, walking past me into the kitchen.

I followed her. "Where have you been?"

"Out."

"Out?" In an instant my fear turned to rage. "*Out?* What do you mean, out? Don't you know you had guests for dinner? Don't you know that you've embarrassed me?"

She didn't answer for a minute or two but sat at the kitchen table like a limp dishrag. Finally she said, "I can't do it, Harald. I'm sorry."

"Can't do what?"

"Feed all those people every Sunday. When they started coming in the front door today, I don't know what came over me, but I just walked out the back."

"Where did you go?" I asked softly.

"An Italian restaurant and then to a friend's." She looked at me, almost pleading with me to understand. "Harald, I can't feed so many people. I can't plan for such crowds. I can't keep cleaning up for so many. There's not even decent work space in the kitchen. I can't ... I can't do it..."

I wanted to put my arms around her and kiss her and say I was sorry. But I couldn't quite forgive her, and I just stood there looking at her.

"Oh, Harald," she began—then started crying, shaking with sobs that lasted so long it was as if they had been stored inside of her for all her life. "And ... I ... can't help you with your ministry or teach the Bible or even take good care of the girls because of all the people you bring home."

Finally I was able to move, to take her in my arms. I could think of nothing to say, but I held her close and let her cry until her tears were all cried out. What a mystery she was to me.

Because I was so sure that it was Gen whom God was going to change, I did not. The extra rooms stayed filled, the guests still kept coming for dinner, and the tension kept mounting between us.

The prayer group was another source of irritation. Gen hated for me to get up early and drive to Brooklyn for the prayer meeting in Dick Simmons's church. I was quietly getting out of bed at five o'clock one January morning when she sat up and snapped on the light. Her voice was as cold as the frost on the windowpanes. "Just where are you going?"

"To the prayer meeting."

"So your wife doesn't matter to you."

"What do you mean?" I asked, groping through a drawer for my socks.

"You know I hate it when you go out in the middle of the night. I wake up and don't even know where you are."

"It's just a prayer meeting."

Her eyes flashed. "It's just your friends coming before your wife! You're not a husband to me, Harald; you've failed me from the day we moved here." She switched off the light and pulled the covers over her head. I knew she had begun to sob.

I wish I had gotten back in bed, put my arms around her and told her the honest truth, that I loved her, and how important her love was to me, but I threw on my clothes, thrust my feet into my shoes, and went downstairs. Instead of going to Brooklyn, I walked across the yard into the icy church. I paced back and forth, shivering in the cold. Over and over I asked myself, "What's the matter with my life? Lord, I *know* You want me to go to the prayer meetings. But what's happening to my marriage? Am *I* at fault?" It seemed incredible that the person I loved most and most wanted to love me was crying because somehow she felt I had failed her. It was too much to bear. As I paced back and forth, I discovered I was crying too.

As much as I ached to do it, I couldn't seem to take the first step that would break down the wall between us. As it and the problems in the church grew, the only comfort I could find was in my old prayer group. Many times they would come up to First Reformed, and we would go over to the stone-walled church, lock the ancient double doors, and really cry out to God. And God did speak to us again and again. Once there was a prophecy that Pat would proclaim the gospel to tens of thousands. Even though it seemed nearly unbelievable, this prophecy came to pass years later when, after prolonged trial and testing, he started the Christian Broadcasting Network, over which he now reaches countless thousands in a single hour. Another word from God was that I would be used as His instrument all over the world—me, the floundering pastor of an obscure church in Mount Vernon. I didn't even share that prophecy with Gen, it seemed so impossible.

Still another word the Lord gave us was that He would produce from an unexpected source the 25,000 dollars we needed to restore the church to its original beauty. A year later we were informed that a 98-year-old agnostic—a total stranger—on his death-bed made out his will leaving us 25,000 dollars.

The word that would directly affect me, Gen, and then our whole church body the most came one night through a message in tongues and interpretation. We were in the choir stall, our favorite spot, praising God, when His message came through my own lips. "On Pentecost Sunday, declare the whole counsel of God. Take no thought for what you are to say, for in that hour it will be given to you. Hold nothing back ... hold nothing back."

I lifted my hands and cried out, "Lord, I'll do it."

Though I knew of only two historic church pastors who spoke in tongues and both had been forced to leave their churches in disgrace, the enthusiasm of the prayer group knew no bounds. The closer the time came, the greater their expectancy. Outwardly I was as gung ho as any of them, but inwardly I was in an agony of doubt.

At two o'clock in the morning on Pentecost Sunday, I came stark awake and knew there would be no more sleep that night. I went over to the church. The moon shone through the rose window, casting shadows across the organ and the divisive pulpit. Up and down the center aisle I paced. The creaking of the floor under my feet and the moaning of the night wind were the only sounds.

"Lord Jesus," I finally cried out, "are You *really* asking this of me? You know what they're going to say: 'We always felt there was something strange about Pastor, and now we know what it is.' They will ask me to leave, and where will I go? Or worse yet, they'll all leave me. Dad warned me, 'Please, don't do anything foolish and jeopardize this chance.' He'll think that is exactly what I've done. So will all my seminary classmates. Everyone will know that Harald Bredesen is a failure."

I sobbed and sank into a pew, my head in my hands.

And then God spoke. *Harald, do you think I care about what mendeem success or failure? Don't you remember the morning I called you?*

Suddenly I was back in my father's church again, and Jesus was speaking to me, only to me: "Harald, lovest thou Me?"

Once again I was overwhelmed by His love for me and my love for Him. Success and failure did not exist. I had but one desire, to give joy to His heart. That was all that mattered.

And then I saw it: that *was* all that mattered—then, now or ever. In that instant, I was delivered from my lifelong bondage to the opinions of other men. I was free! I could almost hear my chains clanking to the floor.

"Hallelujah!" I shouted and kept on shouting in the empty church. Sheer joy brought me to my feet ... and set them dancing.

Imperceptibly a pre-dawn glow had come into the church, and now the first shaft of the rising sun streamed through the rose window and illumined the whole chancel. Never had I seen anything so beautiful!

My heart overflowed with His love. I raised my hands and sang in the Spirit. Then I went forward and knelt at the altar. "Lord Jesus, I *will* declare the whole counsel of God..."

By 11:30, it all seemed a distant dream. Doubt and fear were back, storming the citadel of my resolve. The offering had been taken, the choir had sung ... the moment had come. I looked out at the congregation and wondered if I could even stand up, much less make my way to the pulpit.

For one panicky moment, I wanted to run. "Jesus, Jesus, help me. Jesus, Jesus..."

Suddenly He was there. His love enveloped me. His peace filled me. I walked into the pulpit and began to speak. I simply told them what God had done in my life, the whole story. I kept nothing back.

The people were thunderstruck. As soon as the service was over, they gathered in clusters at the back of the church. Some grouped around my organist, Professor Neilson, and I could hear him saying, "I don't believe for one minute that Pastor's had the experiences that he claims to have had."

Then I heard George Wedlake, of whom I had once said, "Either that man goes, or I go," say, "But, Professor, it's *in the Bible.*"

His words had a calming effect on everyone, and I was filled with hope, hope that made my heart soar. For if the most influential man in the church should appeal to the Bible as the ultimate authority, if we could agree on that, then everything else would fall into place.

And then Gen came up, her eyes glistening, and kissed me on the cheek. And my own eyes moistened as I slipped my arm around her waist.

The following Sunday was Pat's last in our church. He was graduating from seminary. As he gave his final sermon, I sensed that God was going to give me a message in tongues—and the interpretation. For a moment my heart was in my throat. I sat on my chair behind Pat and scanned the faces of our congregation. In their usual places in the choir stall were George and Anna Wedlake. They had accepted my testimony as scriptural, but how would they react to this? There was Bob, the fuel-oil contractor. I wondered if the little knob inside of him was turned off to Pat's preaching, too, and, if so, if it might stay off until I finished.

I looked at Wilson Scott, chairman of our finance committee and our biggest donor. He had once told his Bible class that blood sacrifice was something that the Jews had carried over from the nomadic tribes who sprinkled blood on their tents to appease the moon goddess. If he thought that about the Blood, what would he think about tongues? I saw Dr. Robert Dehaan, the chairman of the Department of Psychology of Hope College, our denomination's largest school. What would he report to our denominational leaders?

And then I remembered. I am free. *Free!* Only one opinion matters: *His.* My heart left my throat, and again I was filled with His peace.

As Pat's message concluded, I opened my mouth, and Jesus filled it. First I spoke in tongues and then gave the interpretation. I don't remember the message. All I remember was the reaction: silence. No, it was stillness. The people were too stunned to even cough.

Only when Professor Neilson started the organ up for the final hymn did the tension break. Reaction ranged from bewilderment to joy to anger. Several walked out and did not return for a year. Yet most of those who had come to Christ under my ministry were thrilled. Two frequent visitors to our church, a wonderful couple, Oscar and Ruth Morris, asked, "Pastor, why have you kept this under a bushel?" And then they added, "We are joining this church, and our friend Ethel Tidmore says she is, too." The church's last remaining dowager said, "I don't know what it was, but when you spoke from the depths of your heart, I was moved almost to tears."

Wilson Scott was really upset. He rushed over to Dr. Dehaan, and within hearing of those around them, asked, "What do you think? Has our pastor gone off his rocker?"

Dr. Dehaan's answer, which included an even wider circle, gave solace, I'm sure, to the Wedlakes, to Gen, and to all those who loved our church and wondered about their pastor: "Something has begun here that I believe is going to revive our whole denomination. How fortunate you are to be in on the ground floor. I covet this experience for myself."

I was grateful for his support, and I regretted Wilson's reaction, but neither of them affected me with the violent swings of emotion that might have been the case even the day before. The important thing was that I had been obedient to the Lord's direction. I had brought joy to His heart, a fact that the unusual peace I felt at the center of the whirlwind confirmed.

More and more I rejoiced in my newfound freedom. Yet it contained a seeming contradiction: It was both fleeting and permanent.

It was fleeting in the sense that it was *not* once-and-for-all; I had continually to re-appropriate it. And it was permanent in that it was *always* there for the taking, instantly available.

Each day I had to claim my liberation, but each day it was there for the claiming.

One morning I awakened with Paul's word to the Galatians running through my mind: "Stand fast therefore in the liberty wherewith Christ hath made us free, and be not entangled again in the yoke of bondage." That Scripture became the lodestar of my life.

When somewhat garbled word got out that our church was becoming Pentecostal, many who had had that experience or were seeking it came.

Some of them showed great love and wisdom in dealing with our people, and as a result, a few parishioners opened up and asked Jesus to baptize them in the Holy Spirit. And so, instead of the failure I had once feared, our church now had a new undergirding of Spirit-filled prayer and financial support. Not only did our total attendance greatly increase, but also our income doubled—this in the face of the catastrophic decline practically all the other old-line Mount Vernon churches were experiencing. There was still, of course, a great deal of unhappiness to be reckoned with, but Jesus was dealing with it.

# 19

One morning at breakfast Gen said, "Harald, you'll have to watch the girls this morning.

"Where are you going?"

"To the doctor's."

"What for?"

"I'm not sure what for, but I know I need to go."

Shortly after lunch, she came home, took off her coat, and sat down in the front room without saying a word.

"What did the doctor say?" I said, glancing up from the desk.

"I have to undergo surgery. I have a tumor."

"A tumor?" The word filled me with dread. *Oh, no, not a tumor,* I thought. *Not Gen.*

"Don't worry. Dr. Winkelstein is sure it's benign."

Eight days after the tumor was removed, Gen was at home recovering in her own bed. I sat beside her, holding her hand and looking at her, crying in my heart for her. She was more beautiful than ever; her dark hair spread out against the white pillow looked like lace. She appeared as fragile as a delicate Russian doll.

As I looked at her, so tiny and helpless, my thoughts went back to a time when I stood beside her on a boat going down the Hudson. All I wanted to do that night was protect her and care for her the rest of my life. Now I had to tell her what Dr. Winkelstein had confided to me that afternoon: that contrary to their initial lab analysis, the tumor *was* malignant, and she would have to undergo surgery again.

Now, as I held her hand, the memories of our last five years raced through my mind. I knew that despite all of our troubles, I loved her beyond reason—and the word "cancer" wouldn't come.

Instead, she talked to me, her voice soft like a child's and sweet. "Harald, I praise God for that tumor, because it has drawn me so close to Him. He has been speaking to me about the faith of Abraham. He has reminded me how Abraham believed and hoped when there was no hope, how his faith in God's promise did not weaken when every natural sign indicated to him that a child by Sarah was out of the question." She paused and gave me a look that was half smile, half question. "Doesn't it seem strange that God should be talking to me about faith, when the tumor turned out to be benign?"

"No, not really strange at all." I had the perfect opening, but I didn't take it. For if I told her, I would have to face it myself. And I couldn't bear the possibility that Gen, my wife, my wife from whom I was still miles apart, might die.

That night I hardly slept. There was such sheer enjoyment lying next to her, feeling the warmth of her body, feeling her hand on my arm ... that I wanted to savor each moment.

The next morning I received a call from Mittie Waters, a dear friend in Raleigh, North Carolina. "Harald, you and Gen have been heavy on my heart this week. I don't know why, but for some reason I'm supposed to share this: Two years ago I had a facial malignancy, but through surgery, God completely healed it. Does that mean anything at all to you?"

I *knew* that this was God's provision for me to tell Gen, and that this time I had to make use of it. "Hang on, Mittie, will you? Wait till I get Gen on the phone."

I called upstairs, "Gen? It's Mittie Waters from Raleigh."

I heard Gen say, "Well, hello, Mittie. How are you? Did Harald tell you? I've just had a tumor removed."

"No, he didn't, but maybe *that's* why you two have been so heavy on my heart. God has been prompting me for two days to call and tell you something." And then Mittie told her the whole story.

"Well, Mittie, that's just wonderful, but *my* tumor wasn't—"

"Gen!" I cut in.

"Yes, Harald?"

"I haven't been able to tell you, but now that God has had Mittie call, I've got to. Dr. Winkelstein called me yesterday afternoon. Gen, honey, your tumor was malignant, and he wants you to return to the hospital for further surgery."

*"Oh, no!"*

"Gen?" It was Mittie's voice, pleading. "You've got to have faith. I *know* God will heal you, just like He did me. Otherwise He wouldn't have laid it on my heart to call you at this time."

"Mittie, I do thank you for sharing, but I ... I can't talk anymore now."

Gen hung up. I thanked Mittie and ran upstairs.

Her face was to the wall.

"Gen, Gen, darling." I cried aloud, "Oh, Jesus, heal Gen, help her, strengthen her. Oh, Jesus, Jesus, Jesus."

Gen spent the next three weeks in the hospital undergoing tests. The night before her second operation, Hal Miller, who was staying with us, burst into my room. "Harald, something's the matter with Meg! She can't seem to breathe."

I jumped out of bed and raced barefoot down the hall. Meg, now two years old, was lying in her crib, tiny and purple-faced, gasping for breath. "Hal, we'd better get her to the hospital."

I drove with Meg beside me on the front seat, choking and whimpering all the way. I was so afraid for her, so helpless. All I could think was, *If only Gen were here, she'd know what to do. What if my baby dies?*

At the local hospital, the doctor discovered something in Meg's trachea, but they didn't have a bronchoscope small enough to remove it. So once more, with Meg beside me, I rushed through the night, this time to Babies' Hospital in Manhattan. At six that morning, the very time Gen was wheeled into surgery, little Meg was on her way to surgery, too. The doctors found a peanut lodged in her trachea.

Word spread rapidly through our church about Gen and Meg.

That Sunday I woke up and for an instant tried to believe it was all a bad dream. Today I really dreaded talking to anyone, especially the people of the church.

As I crossed the grounds, George and Anna Wedlake stopped me first. "Pastor, we're so sorry. What can we do?" There was compassion in George's face and tears in Anna's eyes. I could see they really cared, and it touched me deeply.

Looking past them, I flinched. Coming straight toward me was Wilson Scott, the man who had asked Dr. Dehaan if I was crazy. I whispered, "Okay, Jesus, what do You want?" As I faced him, he put his arm around my shoulder. "I know how hard this must be for you, Pastor. I hope you'll accept a little help from all of us." He handed me an envelope, and in it was a check for a thousand dollars. Like George and Anna and Wilson Scott, everyone I met that morning came to me with love.

I stood in the pulpit and looked at the faces filled with understanding and care. In that moment my heart filled too, filled with love for each of the people of my church. I saw them as they were, each a precious sheep whom God had entrusted to me. And I loved them. When I prayed for my wife and baby I wept openly, and my people wept with me. What I had been trying to do all these years, God did in a moment—His way.

The next day brought news that Meg was out of danger. After that, her recovery became rapid. Daily I went to the hospital to see Gen. The doctors had done all they could, and with every visit we held each other's hands and claimed her complete healing.

One afternoon Gen was asleep when I arrived. I sat down and waited for her to awaken. When she opened her eyes, she asked, "Is the bed still there?"

"Yes, you're lying on it."

"I couldn't feel it. It's Jesus. He's so with me and cushions me so that I can't feel anything but Him. And Abraham, the faith of Abraham, is oozing inside of me and outside. It wasn't strange at all, was it, that God should speak to me about faith?" She closed her eyes and fell asleep again. That day I went home, knowing that Gen would be completely healed.

Several days later I was sitting by her bed and heard her say, "'Thy Maker is thy husband.'"

"What was that, Gen?"

"'Thy Maker is thy husband. The Lord of hosts is His name.' I used to take that Scripture to mean that God would be my husband and that I wouldn't marry. Then God showed me I was to marry you, and I thought I had misunderstood the Scripture, but Harald, 'Thy Maker *is* thy husband.'"

"What do you mean?"

She was asleep again. I sat beside her a long time, looking at her, loving her.

At last Gen was well enough to come home. I had everyone in the house—I couldn't believe there were 14 of them—get the place shipshape, and that night I oversaw the cooking of the meal myself.

Gen smiled and tried to show her appreciation, but she was dreadfully weak, and I put her to bed right away. When she was comfortable, I sat on the edge of the bed; it was our first chance to have some quiet time alone.

"You know, Gen, you said something in the hospital ... I don't know whether you were asleep or awake, but it's been on my mind ever since."

She smiled. "'Thy Maker is thy husband.'"

"That's right, how did you know?"

She leaned back on the pillow and took my hand in hers. "The Lord has been teaching me more than just faith, Harald." She traced over my knuckles with her finger. "When we got married, I transferred the dependence I had on Him to you, but when I was in the hospital, God showed me that *He* is my husband. Oh, Harald, don't you see? He must be my *main* source of comfort and support." She reached up and put her hand on my cheek. "God has done something else for me. The surgeon removed the cancer, and He removed the root of bitterness beneath it."

"Gen, I learned something, too, while you were away. I learned what it was like to look after Meg and Dagni, feed a dozen people, figure out the laundry, do the marketing, and try to keep the place from looking like a flophouse. Then, to top it off, Tim, the kid who ran away when we disciplined him, phoned to ask if he could come back, and guess what I told him?"

"Knowing you, Harald, you said 'Yes, of course.'"

"This will surprise you, Gen—I was surprised myself—but I said no."

Gen giggled and then caught her breath at a stab of pain, then giggled again. And I covered her face with kisses.

"Ahem." I sat up with mock propriety and went on. "You see, God had been speaking to me through a verse in Mark 7, where Jesus rebukes the Pharisees for giving to God the support that they owed their parents. He says, 'God doesn't want stolen gifts.'

"God has been showing me that He doesn't want me to take the time and attention I owe you and give it to Him or anybody else. It's not mine to give. It's yours. But most of all, He has been showing me that the prayer I have been praying for you is the prayer I should be praying for myself."

"What have you been praying for me?"

"That He would change you—open your eyes. He's been showing me that it's my eyes that needed opening. The afternoon that Dr. Winkelstein told me your tumor was actually malignant but not to tell you, I went out into the woods to try to lay hold of God. I felt a terrible sense of doom and hopelessness. It just seemed as if God was going to take you from me, and, sweetheart, when I thought I was going to lose you, I suddenly saw you—really saw you for the first time. I tried to imagine what life without you would be like. Oh, Gen, it was awful!

"Then God began dealing with me. He showed me that He had chosen you for me from all eternity, that He had made you a rarely beautiful person, the one person in all the world who could completeme. He spoke so clearly to me: *I entrusted her to you to cherish and protect. Give an account of your stewardship. What kind of a husband have you been?*

"And then, Gen, He showed me so many areas where I had failed you—crushed you—shut you out—so many. How could I have been so blind? I cried out, 'Oh God, forgive me! Give me another chance! Make me a real husband!'"

And then, weeping, I spoke the words to Gen I had wanted to for so long. "I'm sorry. Forgive me. I love you."

Silent tears fell down her cheeks as she nodded her forgiveness. I put my arm around her and drew her close to me, and together we sat in the quiet for a long time. Then I prayed, "Yes,

Lord, I will be the husband You want me to be. Thank You that You're still opening blind eyes."

Norman, me and Grandma Knutson

Uncle Harold in his Congressionalm portrait.

Aunt Lydia.

My austere, imposing Luther College
antecedents.

The Bredesens, circa 1926

A PR shot of the World Council of Christian
Education's PR whiz.

Be it ever so humber ... 337 Ponce de Leon
Ave., Venice, Florida

My installation as pastor of the First Reformed
Church of Mt. Vernon, New York, with Gen and
George Wedlake looking on.

In His House.

The rose window.

Dagni, 1957

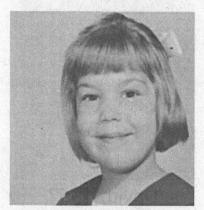

Meg, 1965

Stephen, 1971

Dagni, 1969

David, 1967

At the Royal Albert, backed by Al Malachuk, Pat Robertson, Oral Roberts, Demos Shakarian, Ray Barnett and my future publisher.

# STORIES, TRIBUTES AND MEMORIES

On August 23, 2003, a mix of 500 celebrities, politicians and church and business leaders gathered at the Beverly Hilton in Beverly Hills, California, to celebrate Harald Bredesen's eighty-fifth birthday. A long list of dignitaries, celebrities and ordinary people paraded to the podium to share their stories.

Pat Robertson recalled how Bredesen had taught him about the baptism of the Holy Spirit and later joined the inaugural board of directors of the Christian Broadcasting Network. Benny Hinn recounted how Bredesen had helped shape his early ministry. "There is only one Harald," Hinn said.

"Everyone who knows Harald for five minutes has a Harald story," said entertainer Pat Boone, who called Bredesen a lightning rod in his own life. "He is like the prophet Elisha—just an ordinary guy willing to say yes [to God]." Boone also recounted that toward the end of the birthday celebration, Bredesen pulled him aside and pointed to one of the guests, Senator Sam Brownback of Kansas. "Remember when we prayed for Ronald Reagan?" Bredesen asked. "I have the same feeling about Sam Brownback. Some day he may be president."

Brownback, Los Angeles County Sheriff Lee Baca, *MovieGuide'* s Ted Baehr, cellist Doug McClure, Angel of Reconciliation artist Steven Lavaggi, Los Angeles-area business leader Bert Boeckmann and charismatic pioneer George Otis, Sr., also added their accolades. "He has been an engine of revival," Otis said. Also present to honor Bredesen were actors Erik Estrada, Gavin MacLeod, Jane Russell, Teri Copley and Rhonda Fleming.

Bredesen, in his characteristic style, blew out the candles on his birthday cake (with Boone's help) and joked about how God is still teaching him lessons as he grows older and his memory fades. "He [God] told me, 'Every time you lose another marble, you have to depend more on Me!'"

Since that life-changing day back in 1946 when God told Harald Bredesen to preach to the people on a bus,

stories of him have traveled far and wide. In the following pages, many of those who knew Bredesen best recount their stories and memories of him and tell how this colorful Lutheran pastor from Iowa had an impact on their lives.
Reprinted from magazine, March 2003
Used by permission

# Pat Robertson

## CBN FOUNDER AND PRESIDENT, TELEVISION HOST AND FORMER CANDIDATE FOR PRESIDENT OF THE UNITED STATES

I was invited to the Presidential Prayer Breakfast in Washington, D.C., to speak to the Senate prayer group of which my father was a member. At the end of a meeting, Bob Walker, the ruggedly handsome editor of *Christian Life,* came over to me, chatted a bit, and then asked, "Have you ever heard of the baptism in the Holy Spirit?"

"That's the experience I have been searching for," I replied, but before I could finish my sentence, we were interrupted, leaving me wondering why he would ask me such a question.

I returned to New York, and arriving at Penn Station went directly to the annual banquet of Christian Soldiers, Inc., on whose board I was a member. Seated at the head table with me was an ebullient young minister, Harald Bredesen, who, it turned out, was public-relations director for the Gospel Association for the Blind. I was drawn to him by his warmth of spirit and was delighted when we discovered at the conclusion of the banquet that we were taking the same subway home. We were no sooner seated than with an engaging smile he asked, "Do you know anything about the baptism in the Holy Spirit?"

"Funny you should ask," I replied. "Just today in Washington I met a fellow named Bob Walker, and he asked me the same question."

"Bob Walker!" he exclaimed. "He's one of my best friends. He's just received the baptism. That's why he wanted to share it with you." Harald was exuberant—I was awed by the providence of God.

It was time to leave, and as the doors of the car swished shut behind me and the train roared off into the darkness, I sensed that this crew-cut cleric was destined to play a profound role in my life. I was soon to learn that earlier that evening, on the way to the banquet, he had asked, "Lord, you must have some reason for taking me to this dinner. What is it?" The moment he walked into the room and saw me, it was as if God said, "This man is the reason I have brought you here. He is open to the baptism in My Spirit."

The next week Bredesen appeared at our apartment in Queens. He had ridden a bicycle all the way from College Point through the heavy New York traffic to bring us a book on the baptism in the Holy Spirit. Needless to say, I was deeply impressed by this man's enthusiasm and commitment to Jesus Christ.

Harald began meeting with our prayer group at the seminary, and then in our homes. He also introduced us to a number of other prayer meetings that were being conducted in the area. My hunger for God grew even deeper.

Harald was teaching on the importance of water baptism. I had been baptized as a boy in the Baptist Church back home, but I knew it was not a believer's baptism. So I asked Harald to baptize me, which he did in First Baptist Church of Flushing. I came out of the water fully expecting Jesus to baptize me in the Holy Spirit just as He had been when He came out of the Jordan. But nothing happened.

The next week Harald invited our prayer group to the Flushing Full Gospel Church to meet with Arthur Graves, the pastor.

Our entire prayer group came and was astonished when halfway through the prayer meeting something happened to Harald. Suddenly he leaped to his feet, a torrent of beautiful words in a tongue I had never heard pouring from the depths of his being. To paraphrase Charles Finney, he "literally bellowed out the unutterable gushing of his heart." He seemed to be transported into another realm of experience. I didn't know what had happened to him. I only knew that God had touched his life.

# Don Moen

## WORSHIP MUSIC PIONEER

What can I say about one of my spiritual fathers? There are so many private moments and private prayers that were life changing for me. You could not spend time with Harald and not be changed.

I remember meeting him for the first time. It was October 2003 at the live recording of "Thank You, Lord," which was held at the Regent University Theater adjacent to CBN. After the recording, I was standing on the stage and my good friend John Turver, CBN's Vice President of Marketing, came up to me and said, "Don, I'd like to introduce you to Harald, Pat's [Robertson] oldest board member." I greeted Harald and he said to me, "Young man, that was the most powerful worship experience I have ever had." Then he went on to say, "Can I have breakfast with you in the morning?"

As graciously as possible, I told him that I had a flight early the next morning and it would probably not be possible to meet. Harald wasn't about to give up, which is a characteristic I was to learn about this man. He said, "I'll meet you at 3:00A.M. if necessary!" It's important to remember that I still did not know I was talking to Harald Bredesen. All I knew was that he was Pat Robertson's oldest board member and his name was Harald! It's funny to me now that I look back on it.

The next morning, my wife, Laura, and I met Harald for breakfast at the Founders Inn. As we began to visit over breakfast, I was amazed at this man. He seemed to be looking deep into my heart and soul. He spoke into my wife's life as if he knew her. Finally, a bit embarrassed, I blurted out, "Who are you? What is your last name?" Harald stared at me with his big eyes and then burst out laughing, almost choking on his breakfast! He had assumed I knew who he was. He said, "My last name is Bredesen." I said, "You mean, like, the Bible teacher Harald Bredesen?" Harald burst out laughing again and confirmed that he was indeed Harald Bredesen, the Bible teacher who was one of the pioneers of the Charismatic movement. Pat Robertson was one of his first interns.

I couldn't believe I was sitting across the table from this man. I had read his books and heard stories about him, and now I was having breakfast with him. It was an experience I will never forget. A deep friendship formed that morning—one that would change my life.

Harald asked if he could stay in touch with me, and we exchanged information. A couple of days later, I received the first of many calls from Harald. He asked me, "What do you want me to call you? Brother? Don?" Then he said, "May I call you 'son'?" I realized then that no one had ever called me son, not even my own father. It simply wasn't a term my father used. So, from that day, Harald always called me "son." He would call and say things such as, "Son, when I see you leading worship, I cannot describe the joy it brings to my heart." "Son, the Lord has put you on my heart today and I called to pray with you." These calls happened frequently, sometimes every day. I couldn't always take the time to talk for a long time, but the moments we visited were always uplifting.

Within the first week of meeting Harald, he asked me to fly out to San Diego and drive with him to a favorite retreat in Mexico to spend some time together in prayer. I found myself saying yes to Harald's request. When I got off the phone, I said to my wife, "What did I just do? I agreed to fly from Alabama to San Diego and go to Mexico with an 85-year-old man I hardly know!" It was totally unlike me to do something like this. My wife, Laura, was equally shocked but said she believed I was supposed to go and that this was a divine appointment. It certainly was.

Once there, I realized that I was joining Harald for one of his well-known "prayer walks." Here we were in Mexico, along the beautiful Pacific Ocean, walking and praying, walking and praying. He didn't want to walk slowly, and because I was the younger man, I had to pull him along sometimes. He would pray, and then say to me, "Son, you pray now—in tongues—louder!" Then he would take his turn. We did this two to three times a day throughout the trip. When we got tired, we sat by the pool and had lunch together, and Harald shared from his heart. I wrote down as much as I could, but finally had to put the pencil down and just listen. He told me things that God had shown him about me. He told me that I would find myself meeting people for the first time and feel love pouring out of me toward them. Countless times since the day that Harald prayed this over me, I have had this feeling.

I also remember him saying, "God has given you a golden key to unlock the hearts of world leaders." I thought about that moment earlier this year as I was meeting with President John Kufuor of Ghana. As I met with President Kufuor, I sang the song "God

Will Make a Way," and as I was singing, Harald's words came back to me.

One night, we were sitting in the hotel room and Harald was reading his book to me. Suddenly, he looked at me and said, "Son, I feel I'm supposed to give you an inheritance, a spiritual inheritance. Is that okay?" Of course, I said yes. Oh, how I wish I had recorded those next few moments. It was too holy to pick up a pencil and begin to write. I just sat there while Harald quietly prayed over me and gave me a spiritual inheritance that has affected my life to this day—and will continue to affect my life forever. I miss him. Many times I have called out his name and wished I could hear him call me "son" again.

I started out intending to write a paragraph or two about how this man has influenced my life, but now I find that I could write an entire book about him. I am eternally grateful that our paths crossed and that we became friends. Thank you, Pat and Gordon Robertson, for asking me to sing at CBN, and thank you, John Turver, for introducing me to "Pat's oldest board member." And thank you, Harald, for being a spiritual mentor to thousands around the world, but especially to me.

# Gordon Robertson

### VICE PRESIDENT OF THE 700 CLUB

Where do I start? I could tell so many Harald stories.

Harald only half-joked to me that he knew me since I was in my mother's womb. My parents knew Harald before I was born. He had a huge impact on our family and, though my father might disagree, I really think that there might not have been a CBN if it were not for Harald Bredesen.

And I might not be where I am today if it were not for Harald. In 1994, I had just come back to the Lord. I had quit practicing law and joined Dad in full-time ministry. One day, Harald took me on one of his famous, life-changing walks. I had been contemplating Luke 10:2, in which Jesus had sent out the 72, saying, "Ask the Lord of the harvest, therefore, to send out workers into his harvest field." The verse was burning in my heart, but I didn't know why. At one point in our walk, Harald suddenly stopped, raised his hands and said, "You need to read the Greek. Jesus didn't 'send' them out, He 'drove' them out. You are not being sent out, you are being driven out."

Later, I looked up the Greek. Harald was right. It literally means to "drive out." From that conversation with Harald came the idea to start the Asian Center for Missions, which I led in the Philippines for a number of years. The center has since trained 600 people and sent 250 missionaries into the field. Harald helped train the first class and visited us often.

At first, we would set up appointments for Harald and keep him very busy while he was in the Philippines. But those schedules never worked—God always had other appointments for him. So on one trip, we simply did not make any appointments for him. When he arrived, he was just crushed by the news. "Why?" I asked, scratching my head. "God always comes through for you. Remember the last time you were here?" I saw Harald's response to being without a schedule of appointments as a contrast of great power and anointing with humility.

That night, he prayed loudly in tongues in our backyard—all night long! We slept through it, but our neighbors thought we had a very strange houseguest. Well, that was the trip that Harald met with and prayed for the then-president of the Philippines, Fidel Ramos. He also met with several Supreme Court justices and one of the wealthiest men in the country.

I often tell the story about his meeting the wealthy man, because it is so funny. One morning, a limousine came to pick up Harald. He said he was still tired and asked if he could take some pillows with him. My wife handed him two—nice ones from our couch. Harald was taken to a helicopter and flown off to meet with the wealthy man. When he returned after spending the night, he had forgotten the pillows. So what did he do? He called someone. Some time later, the chauffeured limo came back to our house with two pillows in the back seat. Apparently,

Harald had left them at the wealthy man's house, who in turn had them flown by helicopter and driven by limo. They were nice pillows, but not that nice! Realizing how much it cost to return them, my wife laughed and asked, "Now what do I do with them?"

Harald was one of a kind. I am thankful that he was a friend and that he was bold enough to challenge me to be driven out.

# Janet Fix St. Pierre

### AUTHOR, FORMER ASSISTANT TO HARALD BREDESEN AND ASSISTANT TO PAT BOONE

In my late 20s, having recommitted my life to the Lord after searching in all the wrong places for happiness, I went looking for a job that would have value in the grand scheme of eternity. I didn't want just a "good" job—I'd had good jobs. I wanted to do the Lord's work.

I was the typical Christian single, believing God intended that all people should be married. After all, since Adam and Eve, His creatures were always two by two—even on the Ark. But now that I was nearly 30 and still single, it took personal crises to make me realize that Jesus was who I needed to fill that aching in my heart.

This new commitment to trust God completely to provide for all of my needs was still fresh when a pastor friend told me that a minister he knew needed a secretary. He told me that this minister would be speaking at his church over the weekend and that I should meet him. So I went. The minister was Harald Bredesen. I'd heard of Harald through books such *They Speak with Other Tongues* and *Face Up with a Miracle,* but I never thought I would meet him. In fact, I wasn't too sure about this "charismatic movement" that was moving through mainline churches.

At the potluck before the service, I was seated across the table from him. He was such a jolly, vibrant man, and everyone wanted to talk to him. We tried to talk about a job, but we couldn't finish a sentence without an interruption. Finally, Harald just said,

"Come to my house tomorrow morning and we'll talk."

Early the next morning, I went to his home in Van Nuys, California, to interview for the job. Thinking he would want to test my skills, I took my steno pad so that I would be ready. We talked a few minutes in his home office, and when he saw my pad, he said, "Good, you came prepared. Take this letter." Then he dictated another one, and another one after that. I realized I had the job.

I reported back the next day, and whenever he needed me. I loved watching him go in and out of praising God between sentences of dictation, and sitting at his poolside while he paced around the pool praying. One day on the way to the airport to pick up a friend who was arriving, the singer Judy Collins came on the radio with the song "Bring in the Clowns." Harald immediately prayed that God could save her soul and bring her into the Kingdom. His spontaneity was inspiring.

After I had worked for Harald a few months, he called me at home and said, "Janet, how would you like to be Pat

Boone's secretary?" Well, I knew that he knew Pat Boone—in fact, I had asked him to get me a copy of Pat's book *A New Song*. He did—an autographed copy. But I wasn't sure he was serious about me being Pat's secretary, because he also had a great sense of humor and loved to joke. When I hesitated, he said, "Pat needs a Spirit-filled secretary, and the Lord has told me you're the one." I couldn't argue with him. I knew his track record and that he did hear God's voice. I prayed that I would hear His voice as well.

And so, in less than a week, I met Pat and was hired. Harald said I was his "sacrificial lamb." But he also said that he was like Mordecai and that I was his Esther—I was "in this place for a time such as this."

Harald called me frequently to ask Pat for an introduction to this person or that. They went together with George Otis to pray with then-Governor Ronald Reagan. Then one day, he had an urgent call. God had told him to meet and interview Anwar Sadat, and he needed a letter of introduction from Pat.

I was blessed to type the letter. Although Pat didn't personally know the Prime Minister, Sadat knew Pat's name, and Harald believed it would open the door for him. It did—Harald had a long and meaningful meeting with the Prime Minister, which he believed took root in his soul.

Everyone who knew Harald also knew that he was truly a man of God. He was called "eccentric," sometimes "strange," but I think his childlike innocence and lack of guile is what enabled him to go to people and places where others feared to tread. He was willing to take chances that "normal" people would talk themselves out of. History shows us that the movers and shakers in God's kingdom are those who are unafraid to appear eccentric for the Lord. Harald Bredesen was part of the continuing story of God's using a person who was willing to say, "Yes, Lord."

# Jackie Yockey

### PRESIDENT, HIGH ADVENTURE MINISTRIES

Harald Bredesen was one of my best friends for more than 30 years. An aura of spiritual expectancy surrounded him wherever he went. If someone approached him, he knew it was a divine connection orchestrated by the Lord. He touched the lives of many of the most influential figures of his time, yet he was always available. No one was undeserving of encouragement or prayer. Although he was a prominent minister to world leaders, he was never too busy to pray with a drug addict for salvation.

If you were fortunate to have met Harald, then he probably took you on one of his legendary prayer walks. Any need you expressed brought an instant stop, and then he would look up and cry out, "My Lord and God, what are You saying?" He would look into your face and say, "Your burden is now my burden." He waited with you until he received an answer from the Lord. When you walked with Harald, you felt God's presence.

Hallelujah! Harald's journey on Earth is complete. I know there are throngs of "best friends" who are in heaven or who are looking forward to being in heaven, praising God with Harald.

# David Aikman

FORMER *TIME* MAGAZINE BUREAU CHIEF IN BEIJING

I first met Harald Bredesen in Berlin in 1981, where we were both speakers at a conference called "Jesus, Hope for the 80s." What struck me immediately about Harald were his enthusiasm, humor and effervescent eccentricity. He would be walking down a Berlin sidewalk with you, engrossed in conversation on some aspect of the Lord's work that either of us might have been involved in, and he would stop suddenly, look upward and almost shout out in a very loud voice, "Praise the Lord! Hallelujah!" I would inwardly cringe and out of the corner of my eye try to discern which passersby had decided we were both quite cuckoo. But Harald never skipped a beat in his walking-narrating-God-praising routine.

There were innumerable "Harald stories" that I picked up from friends who had known Harald longer than I had. In one of them, Harald had been invited to speak at an afternoon event on a stage, perhaps at some retreat location. Feeling drowsy because he had been traveling before the event, Harald found a quiet spot beneath the stage for a nap. And nap he did—for such a long time that he missed the entire event and didn't realize it had started over his head without him.

Harald once stayed at our home. He needed to be driven somewhere for a meeting, but he suddenly remembered he hadn't clipped his toenails. So there in the car, driving down the busy streets of northern Virginia, Harald Bredeson, man of God, took his shoes and socks off in the front seat, hauled his left leg up into his lap, and started applying a nail clipper to it.

On the same trip, he decided he hadn't shaved that morning, so out came a battery-powered electric razor, which was soon buzzing away as my wife drove him off to yet another destination. Through all of this he was utterly unselfconscious, laughing as heartily at his own bizarre behavior when it was pointed out to him as were those who were observing it.

Harald was an amazingly humble man. It always surprised me how many people—often quite prominent people—he had not only led to the Lord but also had led into the baptism in the Holy Spirit. Introducing people to the baptism was what Harald seemed to enjoy doing most, and he was remarkably effective at it.

Above all with Harald, his life was seamless: his absent-minded eccentricity, his love of the Lord, his energy for ministry of every kind, his spontaneous and immediate affection for anyone who he thought shared his same divine enthusiasms. Harald will be causing a lot of people to laugh in heaven for a long time.

# Scott Ross

## CHRISTIAN RADIO PIONEER AND TELEVISION BROADCASTER

Like individual leaves on trees or the distinctiveness of a snowflake, each are unique; no two are alike. Harald

Bredesen was the only one of his kind, "fearfully and wonderfully made."

I met Harald in the late 1960s through Pat Robertson in Portsmouth, Virginia, at the then fledgling Christian Broadcasting Network. I had only known Pat for a short period of time when he hired me as a radio disc jockey and sometime co-host of the daily *700 Club.* I was a dripping-wet newly recovered Christian, having spent a number of prodigal years in New York City. I was also recently married to Nedra Talley of the rock and roll group The Ronettes.

As I remember it, my first encounter with Harald was the moment he came bounding into the television studio, with a big smile on his face, arms raised in the air and shouting, "Hallelujah, we love You, Lord!" at the top of his lungs. It didn't seem to matter to him that we were about to go on the air and that breaking into the preparatory silence and countdown to airtime was not the way to do that. But as I got to know Harald over the years, that was par for the course; he seldom played by the rules. He wasn't a rebel; it's just that he marched to the beat of a different drummer. Or, to use a biblical term, Harald went where the wind of the Holy Spirit led him: "Just as you can hear the wind but can't tell where it comes from or where it will go next, so it is with the Spirit" (John 3:8). So it was with Harald.

This was particularly true if one were traveling with Harald or out for a walk with him. Harald loved to walk and talk, and that was an adventure in itself. These spontaneous walks could happen at any time or any place, day or night. Sometimes it would begin with a late-night phone call or after leaving a large teaching conference, his booming voice issuing the invitation, "Let's take a walk, brother!" I remember walking up and down many a staircase or trekking through the woods or down a sandy beach. Time was of no consequence to Harald, and one had to remind him that the rest of the world adhered to a clock and that he was the next speaker at the conference and that we had better get back before they introduced him. He didn't always make it.

And the talks on the walks! Harald had a way of drawing you out into a conversation, and you would find yourself sharing very personal information with him. He would listen to you talk with few comments, other than brief exclamations of, "Thank You, my Lord." At the end of a discourse on some of the foibles of life, one would wait for Harald to respond, which he would do, but not quite in the way one would expect.

"Brother, let's pray!" Harald would exclaim, and rather than wait for your consent, off he would go into a language not known to common man. He was known as "Mr. Charisma" for a reason. Harald would pray in tongues, as described in the New Testament (see Acts 2; 1 Cor. 12; 14). If you didn't pray in tongues, or couldn't join him, you would find yourself a spectator to a man in a very personal prayerful communion with his God. After an indeterminate period of time, Harald would then exclaim loudly, "Thank You, my God," and then begin to give insight into the personal dilemma you had just shared with him.

This similar dynamic of Herald's relationship with the *person* (which he emphasized) of the Holy Spirit came into play in large conferences and small groups that Harald addressed. Declaring the reality of the baptism in the Holy Spirit, Harald spoke with authority and humor that often disarmed his listeners' many theological arguments and questions. He would then make his bottom-line point: "Jesus Christ is the baptizer in the Holy Spirit, and He wants to do that for you now!" Harald would then pray, with the result that the few or even hundreds coming into this biblical experience would find their lives impacted by this man and his message.

That message took Harald to the nations of the earth, before literal kings, princes and presidents, as well as paupers. Harald was a catalyst in bringing many people and factions together as a minister of reconciliation.

Those who knew him loved to share Harald stories together. The conversation would start with, "There was the time that Harald..." and off we would go on another Harald adventure.

One of those times was when Harald was scheduled to appear on a new CBN radio network we were dedicating in upstate New York. Pat Robertson and I and a host of others were waiting for Harald's arrival. No Harald. Minutes before the program was to air, we received a phone call from Harald, wondering where we all were.

"We are in Ithaca at the radio station where you are supposed to be," I said.

"Oh, I see," responded Harald.

"Where are you?" I asked."

"Utica," Harald replied. He was only off by a hundred miles or so. His contribution to the dedication of the new CBN radio network that day was via telephone.

Then there was the time that we set sail with a number of folks from Athens, Greece, on a Mideast tour. Harald was one of the tour guides for the trip. When the ship set sail from Athens ... no Harald. Although his always faithful, patient wife, Gen, was on board with us, we had no idea where he was. Gen didn't seem to be too worried about him. Harald's disappearances were not new to her.

A few days later as we were clambering among some tombs in the biblical city of Philippi, all of sudden we heard shouts of, "Praise God! There you are!" From among the dead of Philippi popped out our very own living tour guide, Harald. It was not until later that Harald explained he had met a group of Greeks in the streets of Athens and engaged them in a conversation. He then went about explaining the way of Jesus to this group (very reminiscent of the apostle Paul) and subsequently prayed with them to meet this Christ who had seemingly directed the steps of Harald and his new converts to this sovereign moment. For Harald, this encounter took precedence over being a tour guide.

To this day, I still don't know how Harald caught up with us at the tombs of Philippi!

My last personal time with Harald was at a dinner in Hollywood, California, to honor Pat Boone. I had been asked to emcee the event. I took the opportunity to not only honor Pat Boone but also Harald, who was in attendance due to the fact that he had had a profound spiritual influence in Pat Boone's life.

Following the gala evening, Harald approached me and, as he was wont to do, linked his arm in mine and invited me "to take a walk." As we ambled through the glitzy lobby of the Hollywood Hills hotel, I asked Harald where we were going. "I don't know," he responded. "I thought you might know the way to the restroom!" And he laughed.

It was the last time I could serve him. Harald Bredesen was with Jesus two weeks later.

# Ted Baehr

**FOUNDER AND PUBLISHER OF MOVIEGUIDE® AND CHAIRMAN OF THE CHRISTIAN FILM & TELEVISION COMMISSION**

Harald Bredesen was one of the giants of the Christian faith over the last century. He changed the hearts and minds of countries, kings and cab drivers.

When I met Harold, I was immediately taken with his Spiritfilled conversation that was always peppered with long spontaneous prayers. He would talk for a moment, break into prayer, and then go right back to talking. Talking to Harald was like peering behind the veil between heaven and Earth and watching him converse with God on His throne.

Harald's prayers were often answered in magnificent ways. He once came to the Annual MovieGuide Faith and Values Awards Gala and said, "You are giving the entertainment industry executives church." Because we were short of the total funding needed, Harald said to us, "I will bring you the funding." We all treated the statement as one of Harald's exuberant encouragements, until the funding was actually received shortly thereafter from his source.

Harald was a man of vision and a man of faith, but more than that, he was a man who walked with God.

# Teri Copley

PRESIDENT OF SONSET MINISTRIES, WRITER, AND ACTRESS OF *THE JOURNEY OF THE SHULAMITE*

I first met Harald at a Benny Hinn crusade. He sat near the front with me and some friends and prophesized like he had known me forever. Like so many others, he invited me to his house to meet his wife, Gen.

Not too long after the crusade, a friend and I went to Harald's house in Escondido, California. We were not there long when Harald announced, "Let's go on a prayer walk!" He wanted us to join him at what has become known as Prayer Mountain, a place where God often touched those who made the journey to the top with Harald. I was game to go, but I had to borrow Gen's tennis shoes.

The three of us—Harald, my friend and myself—hiked up the mountain. It was huge and took 45 minutes or so to climb. I am not a hiker, so I was thinking, *Okay, Harald, you are an* awesome man of God. But when is this going to end?

When we finally got to the top, there was no great view or lake.

It was just a simple mountaintop. So what was it that was so special about this place? I was about to find out. Harald, in his simple and elegant way, offered an innocent hug. I was uncomfortable receiving this childlike hug ... silly as that sounds ... and my first thought was not too spiritual: How do I tell this precious man no?

Of course, I could not. So the three of us hugged. Let me make it clear that it was very appropriate and respectful, and at that moment, God broke something within me. You see, Harald broke through the human veils. He did not adhere to manmade boundaries, which is what made him so precious and innocent. Harald respected people, but he respected God more.

We said a little prayer, nothing showy or grandiose. Then we went and picked up some Chinese food. Oh, and Harald fell asleep in the car on the way home, which will not come as a surprise to anyone who knew Harald.

During that ride home, I quietly started crying. I had never known that kind of innocent, pure and even childlike love, and through Harald, God had shown it to me on the mountaintop. In that moment, I knew the gift of God's love.

Harald came to call himself my spiritual father, and there were many times when he spoke words of power, encouragement, counsel and prophecy directly into my heart. But I will always remember that first hike to Prayer Mountain.

# Bill Hamon

FOUNDER OF CHRISTIAN MINISTRIES INTERNATIONAL NETWORK, PROPHET AND AUTHOR

Harald was one of the most unique men of God I have ever known. He had anointing to touch key leaders of the church—he was a real prophet of God. He was a great man of vision and boldness. He would meet you, pray for you and end up leading you to the Lord. It didn't matter if you were a world leader or the waiter at a restaurant.

Some people might say that he operated like an absent-minded professor, but he really demonstrated the confidence and simplicity of faith. Harald empowered me to be bolder. He influenced me with his vision, his faith and his ability to hear the voice of God in all circumstances.

You only meet a few people like him in your life. For Harald, it was simple: If God said it, then he was going to do it.

# Wendy Griffith

### SENIOR REPORTER, CBN NEWS
### CO-ANCHOR, CBN *NEWSWATCH*

On a Sunday morning in early May 2004, then 85-year-old Harold Bredesen asked me if I would drive him to the train station in Newport News, Virginia. He was going to New York City—an 8-hour journey by train. The train station was about a 45-minute drive from Virginia Beach where we were. I said sure.

When we arrived, I parked my car illegally outside the train station because we were late and helped him board his heavy suitcase onto the train. We'd only been inside the train a few seconds when it started to move. I thought, *This can't be, surely they give you time to get situated.* But the train was indeed moving out of the station, and it looked as if I were along for the ride.

Suddenly, I had a sense this was not an accident—that perhaps God wanted me to go along to help Harald. After all, he was 85 and traveling alone all the way to New York City, and the food car was several train cars away. Harald also felt this was a divine appointment, and so by the time we passed Richmond and Washington, D.C., I was invested. I confessed to the train attendant that I was a stowaway, and Harold bought me a ticket in D.C. (they were also able to push my car out of the illegal area).

As it turned out, Harald did need a lot of help on that trip. His suitcase was heavy, and he needed me to get it down from the rack several times. I was also able to get his lunch. I remember that he drank milk with his sandwich. But mostly, he needed someone to practice his sermon on that he intended to give that night at Morning Star Church in New York City. I felt humbled and privileged. After all, Harold was an institution. I knew a little about how his encouragement to Pat Robertson had helped him launch the Christian Broadcasting Network. The list of people he'd ministered to included presidents and world leaders. And he wanted *me* to listen to his sermon?!

What made the trip even more intriguing was that Harald thought that the man who planned to pick him up at Penn Station in New York that day might be my future husband. Being single, I was open to the idea—especially since it was coming from Harald Bredesen. Harald told me that the guy was a Christian and very handsome.

I thought that his idea of handsome and my idea of handsome might be two totally different things, but as turns out, Harold was right—and then some. This guy (we'll call him Frank) and I really hit it off, and we had what turned into a three-month summer romance. I couldn't help feeling a bit like Rebecca being led by Abraham's servant on her way to meet Isaac.

I'll never forget that trip with Harald. It was eight hours well spent—and even led to a summer romance. Thanks, Harald! I'd love to travel with you again someday...

# Merlin Carothers

### AUTHOR OF *THE POWER OF PRAISE*

Many years ago, I occasionally had the joy of meeting Harold at his home in Escondido, California. I would join him on his daily, early morning walk. During those times, I asked about his meetings with foreign dignitaries and why he thought he had been given these unusual opportunities. Harald always said that he could not explain *why* God had chosen him to be used to minister to kings and heads of nations.

My own conclusion was that Harold had the heart and desire, without hesitation or reluctance, to speak to *anyone* about Jesus. Few people have such a special gift. He had the ability to witness to servants and heads of state in his own loving, uninhibited way. I believe they listened because they sensed that his words were from his heart.

# Tom Gilbreath

CHAIRMAN OF THE BOARD OF DIRECTORS OF CHARISMA MINISTRIES

Around 1973, my family signed up for cable television. I was thrilled. With cable, we would receive almost a dozen channels. Television had at last arrived. Now I was sure there would always be something good on ... and I wasn't as far wrong as you might think.

Those were the days before cable companies received their signals from satellites, so the extra channels tended to be regional ones. I was in Lubbock, Texas, and our cable gave us a couple of Dallas stations, including KXTX, which was owned at that time by CBN. To the delight of my then teenage heart, it ran *Star Trek* five days a week. But another program also caught my attention: *The700 Club.* With its dynamic young host, Pat Robertson, this was TV like I had never seen before. I watched it as often as I could.

Another Christian talk show immediately followed—*Charisma.* I watched *Charisma* during the time it took me to get off the couch, go to the television and hit the on-off switch. I didn't give it a chance. The host, Harald Bredesen, wore a clerical collar, something I associated with stuffiness. Also, there was more luminance in his demeanor than I had experienced, so I judged it too brilliant to be real.

I met Harald in 1984 and then reread two books that had been especially influential in my life, *The Cross and the Switchblade* by David Wilkerson and *Shout It from the Housetops* by Pat Robertson. At pivotal moments in both books, there was Harald, my new friend. I found him in other books, too, such as Pat Boone's *A NewSong* and John Sherrill's *They Speak with Other Tongues.* Again and again, Harald's story was integral to the testimonies of other prominent Christians.

Harald often said, "God inhabits eternity but has a marvelous sense of timing." He knew this from his own experience. I worked as his assistant from January of 1985 until his death in December 2006. (In many ways, I'm still at it.) I saw the scenario played out repeatedly. God placed Harald at just the right place and time to have maximum impact on key people at crucial points in their lives.

This was true for individuals. I believe it was also true for the Church as a whole. The first mainline churchman to receive the baptism in the Holy Spirit and remain a mainline churchman, Harald brought Pentecostal doctrine and freedom of worship across the tracks into the nice part of town, to "respectable" denominations and upscale congregations. Today, that influence permeates Christian assemblies of all socio-economic levels around the world.

In the months since he left us, I've gone through a mountain of old materials, uncovering many treasures.

I'm especially excited any time I come across a videotape labeled *Charisma.* I put the tape in the machine, turn on the television, and there sits the man with the collar. He smiles, and I'm warmed again by the Son shining through his face.

# Stephen Baldwin

ACTOR AND FOUNDER OF THE GLOBAL BREAKTHROUGH MINISTRY (WWW.GLOBALBTM.COM)

I remember the first time I met Harald. It was at Pat Robertson's seventy-fifth birthday party. I was quietly waiting to greet Pat when I heard a loud voice off to one side. I looked over and saw this short man greeting some people, looking up into their faces, doing whatever he could to make eye contact—and expressing deep sentiments about the Lord. *Who is this guy?* I thought. I was curious. I had to know more, so I strolled closer and stood nearby until Harald noticed me.

"Oh my goodness," Harald said as he looked up into my eyes. "The joy of the Lord is all over you!"

From those words, a friendship grew. As I listened and watched Harald, I knew that whatever he had in his relationship with the Holy Spirit, I wanted. Our walk with the Lord should be full of peace and joy that comes from truly loving Jesus. I can honestly say that I have met a lot of people—good Christians—but I have never met anyone who was having that experience in as great or more intimate a way than Harald. He was just full of the Spirit, and it was infectious.

As I got to know Harald better, I saw more of how he reflected the joy of the Lord toward me (and everyone around him). He was an example of actually allowing the Holy Spirit to work through him in a way that most of us just talk about. I felt a bit of an impartation into my heart—an imparting of that more intimate touch. Because of Harald and others like him, today I have a far greater understanding and heart knowledge of the intimacy of the Holy Spirit.

# Pat Boone

## LEGENDARY ENTERTAINER AND COAUTHOR OF *THE CULTURE-WISE FAMILY*

I was being honored for my support of a Jewish hospital in Israel and was astonished to see Harald walk into the gathering in Beverly Hills, California. Of course, he was welcome, though his presence was unexpected. Then again, knowing Harald, nothing should have been a surprise. As you have read, when led by the Holy Spirit, he would just pop in on kings, presidents, pastors, movie stars—just about anyone. Years ago, Harald showed up at my house with a clear message from God. If I had not listened and followed his advice, my marriage might have come apart and my career might have faded away.

Harald and I had many great times together. One in particular stands out. It was on the night when George Otis, Sr., Keith Phillips, Harald and I prayed with then-California governor Ronald Reagan and George prophetically suggested that Reagan might some day occupy 1600 Pennsylvania Avenue. That night in Beverly Hills, Harald was stooped and a bit frail, but inside he was the same person I had known for four decades. He was vigorous, loving and full of the Holy Spirit. We talked briefly and hugged each other, not knowing that would be the last time we would see each other.

This photo, taken by a dear friend at that gathering, captures us together at the gathering in Beverly Hills, just days before Harald went on to his greater reward in heaven.

FOR MORE INFORMATION
ABOUT HARALD BREDESEN AND
CHARISMA
MINISTRIES, LOG ON
TO HARALDBREDESEN.COM
OR WRITE TO:

**CHARISMA MINISTRIES**

P.O. BOX 460395
ESCONDIDO, CA 92046-0395

# More from Regal Books

**The Supernatural Life**
Experience the Power of
God in Your Everyday Life
*Cindy Jacobs*
ISBN 978.08307.37030

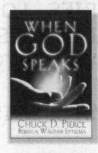

**When God Speaks**
How to Interpret Dreams, Visions,
Signs and Wonders
*Chuck D. Pierce and
Rebecca Wagner Sytsema*
ISBN 978.08307.37073

**Freedom From the
Religious Spirit**
Understanding How Deceptive
Religious Forces Try to Destroy
God's Plan and Purpose
for His Church
*C. Peter Wagner*
ISBN 978.08307.36706

**God's Unfolding Battle Plan**
A Field Manual for Advancing
the Kingdom of God
*Chuck D. Pierce*
ISBN 978.08307.44703

**The Future War
of the Church**
How We Can Defeat Lawlessness
and Bring God's Order to the Earth
*Chuck D. Pierce and
Rebecca Wagner Sytsema*
ISBN 978.08307.44142

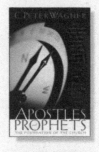

**Apostles and Prophets**
**The Foundation of the Church**
Biblical Leadership
for the 21st Century
*C. Peter Wagner*
ISBN 978.08307.25762

# FRONT COVER FLAP

Yes, LORD!

INCLUDES STORIES, MEMORIES AND
TRIBUTES FROM:

DAVID AIKMAN

TED BAEHR

STEPHEN BALDWIN

PAT BOONE

MERLIN CAROTHERS

TERI COPLEY

JANET FIX ST. PIERRE

TOM GILBREATH

WENDY GRIFFITH

BILL HAMON

DON MOEN

GORDON ROBERTSON

PAT ROBERTSON

SCOTT ROSS

JACKIE YOCKEY

# BACK COVER FLAP

## HARALD BREDESEN
### (1918-2006)

was a Lutheran minister who became one of the most influential ministers in the early days of the Charismatic Movement. Known by many as "Mr. Charisma," Bredesen was involved in the founding of major Christian media ministries, including the Christian Broadcasting Network, Trinity Broadcasting Network, and 100 Huntley Street in Canada. Over the years, Bredesen's ministry was featured on ABC, the BBC, *Radio Moscow,* CBS's *The World Tonight* and Walter Cronkite's *News and World Report,* as well as other major international news programs. Articles chronicling his ministry and influence were featured in *Time, The Saturday Evening Post, Encyclopedia Britannica, Charisma Magazine and Christianity Today.* Bredesen was the author of the bestselling book *Need a Miracle?*

# BACK COVER MATERIAL

DISCOVER WHAT HAPPENS WHEN YOU
SAY, "YES, LORD"

"PREACH TO THE PEOPLE ON THIS
BUS."

"But, Lord, I can't! Lutheran ministers
don't preach on buses in the middle of
Manhattan! They'll think I'm—"

"DO IT. NOW."

From that life-changing day on the bus
to meetings with presidents and kings,
stories of Harald Bredesen's adventures
in the Lord have traveled far and wide.
Who was this unassuming, faithful
follower of Christ who fought against
following in his preacher father's
footsteps? Come hear from the man
himself—Harald Bredesen—who learned
the ups and the downs of learning to
say, "Yes, Lord," no matter what. This
story of a young man's growing pains
in Christ becomes the story of a man
who would one day find himself in the

company of world leaders and who would one day become an important influence in the lives of many prominent people, including Pat Robertson, Gordon Robertson, Pat Boone, Wendy Griffith, Scott Ross, Teri Copley, Jackie Yockey, and others. Sit back and let Harald tell his almost unbelievable stories of how he was willing to be led to the right place at the right time, where he was often given just the right words. And it all started with him saying, "Yes, Lord."